**Tipbook Trumpet & Trombone,
Flugelhorn and Cornet**

Publishing Details

This first edition published November 2001 by
The Tipbook Company bv, The Netherlands.

Distributed exclusively by the Hal Leonard Corporation,
7777 West Bluemound Road, P.O. Box 13819,
Milwaukee, Wisconsin 53213.

Typeset in Glasgow and Minion.

Printed in The Netherlands by Hentenaar Boek bv, Nieuwegein.

The publisher and author have done their best to ensure the
accuracy and currency of all the information in the Tipbook,
however, they can accept no responsibility for any loss, injury or
inconvenience sustained as a result of information or advice
contained in the guide. Trademarks, user names, and certain
illustrations have been used in this book solely to identify the
products or instruments discussed. Such use does not identify
endorsement by or affiliation with the trademark owner(s).

© 2001 THE TIPBOOK COMPANY BV

144pp

ISBN 90-76192-41-3

Hugo Pinksterboer

Tipbook
Trumpet &
Trombone,
Flugelhorn & Cornet

Handy, clearly written, and up-to-date.
The reference manual for both beginners and advanced
brass wind players, including Tipcodes and a glossary.

THE **TIPBOOK**
COMPANY

THE BEST GUIDE TO YOUR INSTRUMENT!

Thanks

For their information, their expertise, their time, and their help we'd like to thank the following musicians, teachers, technicians, and other brasswind experts: Donald R. Harrell (Kanstul, CA), Max Gastauer (B&S, Germany), Jeff Christiana and Kelly Edwards (UMI, IN), Brock M. Scutchfield (Woodwind & Brasswind, IN), Bernd Limberg (Gewa, Germany), Frits Damrow (Conservatory of Amsterdam), Jarmo Hoogendijk (Nueva Manteca, Conservatories of The Hague and Rotterdam), Bart van Lier (Conservatories of Amsterdam and Rotterdam), Carina ter Beest, Kik Boon, Luc Decock, Gerald van Dijk, Harm van der Geest, Bart Noorman, Bert Reuyl, Henk Rensink, Louis Schuijt, Henk Smit, Harry Thoren, Diana Voorhof, Hans de Winter, Jacob Bakker, Paul van Bebber (First Brass), Aad Contze (Selmer/ BIN), Pieter Bukkems and Harm Roestenberg (Holton, Martin/ JIC), Guus Dohmen, Harry Thoren, Gerard ten Hoedt and Jeroen Bos, Gerard Koning (Yamaha), Dirk de Moor (Musik Meyer), Bart Noorman, Jan Otten, Henk Rensink, Tom Reitsma, Jaap Ruisch (Van der Glas), Jan Slot, and Richard Steinbusch (Adams). We also wish to thank BIN (Selmer), JIC (Holton), Musik Meyer (Jupiter), and UMI (King) for supplying instruments for this book.

Anything missing?

Any omissions? Any areas that could be improved? Please go to www.tipbook.com to contact us; thanks!

Acknowledgements

Concept, design, and illustrations: Gijs Bierenbroodspot

Cover photo: René Vervloet

Translation: MdJ Copy & Translation

Editor: Robert L. Doerschuk

Proofreader: Nancy Bishop

IN BRIEF

Have you just started playing? Are you thinking about buying a trumpet, a trombone, a flugelhorn, or a cornet, or do you just want to know more about the one you already have? If so, this book will tell you all you need to know. About buying or renting instruments, lessons and practicing, play-testing brass instruments, choosing mouthpieces and mutes, maintenance and tuning, about the history and the family of brasswind instruments, and much more besides.

The best you can

Having read this Tipbook, you'll be able to get the most out of your instrument, to buy the best instrument you can, and to easily grasp any other literature on the subject, from magazines to books and Internet publications.

Begin at the beginning

If you have just started playing, or haven't yet begun, pay particular attention to the first four chapters. Have you been playing any longer? Then skip ahead to Chapter 5. Please note that all prices mentioned in this book are mere indications of street prices in American dollars.

Glossary

The glossary at the end of the book briefly explains most of the terms you'll come across as a brass player. To make life even easier, it doubles as an index.

Hugo Pinksterboer

CONTENTS

SEE WHAT YOU READ WITH TIPCODE

www.tipbook.com

In addition to the many illustrations on the following pages, Tipbooks offer you an additional way to see – and even hear – what you are reading about. The Tipcodes that you will come across regularly in this book give you access to extra pictures, short movies, soundtracks, and other additional information at www.tipbook.com.

How it works is very simple. One example: On page 98 of this book you can read about how to use a cloth to remove a valve slide. Right above that paragraph it says **Tipcode TRP-019**. Type in that code on the Tipcode page at www.tipbook.com and you will see a short movie that shows you this technique.

Enter code, watch film

You enter the Tipcode beneath the movie window on the Tipcode page. In most cases, you will then see the relevant images within five to ten seconds. Tipcodes activate a short movie, sound, or both, or a series of photos.

Tipcodes listed

To make it easy, you can find all the Tipcodes used in this book in a single list on page 126.

Quick start

The Tipcode movies, photo series, and sound tracks are designed so that they start quickly. If you miss something the first time, you can of course repeat them. And if it all happens too fast, use the pause button beneath the movie window.

First, make your selection: Tipcode, chords and fingering charts, or the glossary.

The Tipcode window displays movies, photo series, fingering charts, chords, and explanations of the words used in this book.

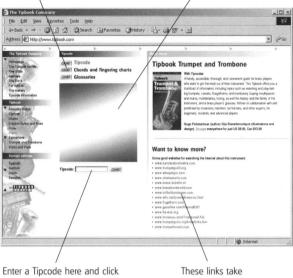

Enter a Tipcode here and click on the button. Want to see it again? Click again.

These links take you directly to other interesting sites.

Plug-ins

If the software you need to view the movies or photos is not yet installed on your computer, you'll automatically be told which software you need, and where you can download it. This kind of software (*plug-ins*) is free.

Still more at www.tipbook.com

You can find even more information at www.tipbook.com. For instance, you can look up words in the glossaries of all the Tipbooks published to date. For clarinetists, saxophonists, and flutists there are fingering charts, for drummers there are the rudiments, and for guitarists and pianists there are chord diagrams. Also included are links to some of the websites mentioned in the *Want to Know More?* section of each Tipbook.

1. A BRASS PLAYER?

If you play the trumpet, that makes you a brass player. Trumpets, trombones, flugelhorns, and cornets – they're all brasswind instruments, and all them can be used in a wide variety of bands and orchestras, and in many different musical styles.

On a guitar the strings vibrate. On a drum the heads do. And on brasswind instrument it's your lips. Just put them together and press air through them – and you can make this sound like air escaping from a balloon, or a motorbike, or... In the same way, you can make a brasswind instrument sound many different ways. From high to low, from crisp, bright, and edgy to warm, soft, and smooth.

Trumpeters and trombonists Tipcode TRP-001

As a trumpet or trombone player you can play in a jazz band, a symphony orchestra, or a brass band; you can join a salsa band, a chamber orchestra, or play with a mariachi band, or in many other groups and ensembles.

Flugelhorns Tipcode TRP-002

The flugelhorn, which sounds fuller, warmer, and mellower than a trumpet, is often played by jazz and classical musicians – sometimes by specialists, but more frequently by trumpet players.

Cornets

The sound of a cornet is somewhere between that of a flugelhorn and a trumpet. It's brighter than the first, but not as bright as the latter – it's mellower than the latter, but not as mellow as the first. Cornets are played in brass bands, of course, and they're also used in Dixieland bands and symphony orchestras.

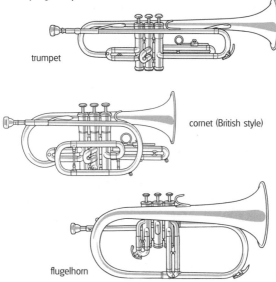

The cornet is somewhere between a flugelhorn and a trumpet.

Orchestras and bands

There's more about the various orchestras and bands you can join as a brass player in Chapter 14 of this book.

Horn

Brasswind players have at least one thing in common: Whether they play a cheap factory-made instrument or a hand-crafted gem, they are likely to call it their *horn*. Incidentally, the same word is used by saxophonists too – even though that's a woodwind instrument (see Chapter 11, *The Family*).

It looks deceivingly simple: a trombone.

Three buttons or a slide

Learning to play a few basic songs or melodies on a brass instrument is a matter of months – but they're not the easiest instruments to learn. They do look deceivingly simple, with just three 'buttons' or one long slide, but that only makes learning to play the instrument harder: You have to produce all the notes yourself.

Just your instrument

Some good things? Brasswind instruments are quite affordable, and it won't cost you a fortune to buy a decent instrument that you can enjoy for many years. Besides, brass players don't need to replace (or buy…) strings, reeds, batteries, heads, sticks or picks. All you need is your instrument, a mouthpiece, a case, and the odd drop of oil – and this book tells you all about it.

2. A QUICK TOUR

The four instruments in this book are similar to each other in many ways. That goes especially for the trumpet, the cornet, and the flugelhorn, of course. A trombone looks more different than it really is. This chapter explains the basics of these instruments, their differences and similarities, and what their main parts are and what they do.

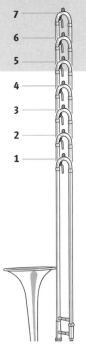

7
6
5
4
3
2
1

Gradually longer in seven steps.

Trumpets and trombones are more alike than you might think. A trumpet is a long tube with three *valves*; a trombone is a long tube with an extendable *slide*. You need those valves or the slide to be able to play all the different notes.

A few notes   Tipcode TRP-003

On a brass instrument without valves or a slide you can only play a limited number of notes, known as the *harmonics* or *naturals*. You can't play everything you want with just those notes.

A little longer, a little lower

By using the slide or the valves you can make the instrument a little longer, step by step. Making it longer makes it sound lower, a half-tone (half-step) at a time. And each time you do, you get access to a whole series of new notes.

Seven steps, seven series

It's easy to see that a trombone gets longer when you extend the slide. It does so in seven steps, from fully retracted to fully open. That means you can play seven 'series' of seven or eight notes. Together, those notes allow you to play anything you want.

Valves

A trumpet works in basically the same way. The three valves allow you to do the same thing as the slide of a trombone: You make the tube a little longer each time, in seven steps. Here's how.

Without valves

If you don't use the valves, the air passes through the main tube of the instrument only. It goes from the mouthpiece to the valves, and from the valves directly to the bell. Without using the valves, you can play some seven or eights harmonics only.

Second valve: a half-tone lower   Tipcode TRP-004

If you use the second valve, the air also passes through the small U-shaped tube attached to the valve. This makes the

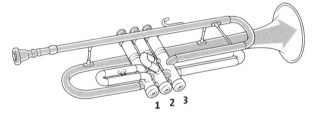

Through the main tube only: The notes you can play without using your valves include Middle C (C4), G4, C5, and E6.

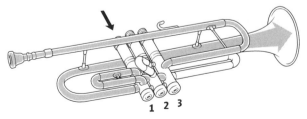

The extra length added by the first valve makes the instrument sound a whole tone lower. Now you can play B-flat below Middle C and an octave up, F4, D4...

tube of the trumpet slightly longer, enabling you to play a new series of notes, which sound a *half-tone lower.*

First valve: two half-tones lower
The U-shaped tube of the first valve, closest to the mouthpiece, is about twice as long as the tube of the second valve. If you depress the first valve, you can play a series of notes which sound *two half-tones* lower than the ones without valves.

Third valve: three half-tones lower
The tube attached to the third valve is about as long as the combined tubes of the first and second valves. Using this valve allows you to play a series of notes which sound *three half-tones lower* than the ones without valves.

Seven positions
Back to the trombone: A trombone slide that is fully retracted is in the *first position.* The *seventh position* means it's fully open. Similarly, the three valves of a trumpet allow for seven 'positions.'

The numbers
These seven 'positions' are indicated with numbers: 0 means not using any valves, 1 means the first valve is depressed. If you want to extend the trumpet step by step, as if you were moving out a trombone slide step by step, here's the order of the valves to use: 0 (no valves/first position); 2; 1; 1+2 (or 3 on its own); 2+3; 1+3; 1+2+3 (all valves/seventh position).
The three valves on a flugelhorn or a cornet work in exactly the same way.

TRUMPET
So a trumpet is really a very basic instrument: a long tube with two bends, and three valves that allow you to vary its length – so you can play everything you want. If you take a closer look, there is much more to see.

Mouthpiece
Brasswinds are *lip-vibrated instruments*: You play them by vibrating your lips in the cup of the *mouthpiece.*

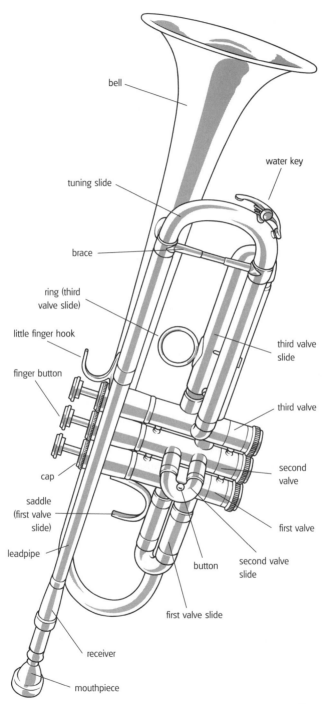

bell

water key

tuning slide

brace

ring (third valve slide)

little finger hook

finger button

third valve slide

third valve

cap

second valve

saddle (first valve slide)

first valve

leadpipe

second valve slide

button

first valve slide

receiver

mouthpiece

Leadpipe

The mouthpiece sticks into the *mouthpiece receiver*, often just called receiver. The next piece of tubing, up till the first bend, is the *leadpipe* or *mouthpipe*. A tip: 'Leadpipe' is pronounced as 'leed-pipe'.

Tuning slide

You tune a trumpet by pulling out the first bend of the instrument, at the end of the leadpipe. If you extend this *main tuning slide* or *tuning crook*, you make the instrument a little longer. As a result the pitch will become a little lower.

The third valve slide

Past the tuning slide, you come to the third valve. The piece of tubing attached to it is the *third valve slide* or *third slide*.

Fine-tuning

You can extend the third valve slide by using the attached *slide throw ring*. This allows you to fine-tune certain notes while playing.

The first valve slide

Many instruments allow for adjusting notes with the first valve slide too. There may be a ring for that purpose, or a U-shaped *thumb hook* or *saddle*, also known as *U-pull*.

Buttons and caps

You operate the valves with *finger buttons*, which are often inlaid with real or imitation mother-of-pearl.

Pistons and valve casings

The trumpet's valves are known as *piston valves*: In each *valve casing*, there's a *piston*, a small cylinder with holes. If the piston is up, the air passes straight through the valve, taking the 'short route.'

Piston down

If you move the piston down, you force the air to make a detour through the valve slide. This makes the tube longer, allowing for a new series of notes. The difference between the short route and the detour is clearly shown in the illustrations on page 5.

Valve caps

To allow the valves to move smoothly, they need to be lubricated. To do so, you can take out the pistons by unscrewing the *valve caps*.

The bell

The *bell* is at the end of the trumpet, but it also includes the last bend: The bell section actually starts at the *bell tail*, just after the valve section.

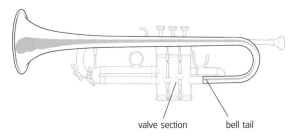

valve section   bell tail

The bell starts right after the valve section.

Braces

Braces between the bell and the leadpipe make the trumpet a little sturdier. Usually there's another brace just before the tuning slide, and there may be one in the tuning slide as well.

Little finger hook

When you play, the index, middle, and ring fingers of your right hand are on the finger buttons. Your right hand little finger is in the hook on top of the leadpipe.

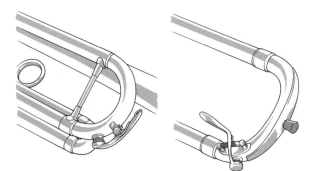

Water keys on a trumpet and a trombone.

Water keys

As you play, the moisture from your breath will condense inside the instrument. To get rid of it, just press the *water key*, blow through your horn noiselessly, and it's gone. Water keys are also known as *spit valves*.

Lyre holder

Marching musicians attach their sheet music to their instrument with a *lyre*. If your horn doesn't have a lyre holder, you can get a lyre that you clamp onto the instrument. Other lyres attach to the holder of the third valve slide ring. This will, however, disable the use of this slide for fine-tuning.

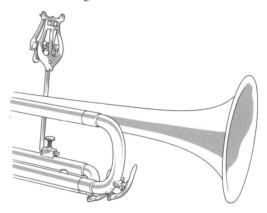

Lyre attached to the holder of the third valve slide ring.

FLUGELHORN

On a flugelhorn, the bends in the tube are much less sharp than on a trumpet. This makes it look 'rounder,' and the instrument also sounds 'rounder' than a trumpet.

Narrow to wide

The round, mellow or velvet sound of a flugelhorn, compared to a trumpet, is mainly due to the fact that a flugelhorn is narrower at the beginning, and much wider at the end. In technical terms: A flugelhorn has a more *conical bore* than a trumpet.

Tuning

You tune a flugelhorn by sliding its short, straight tuning

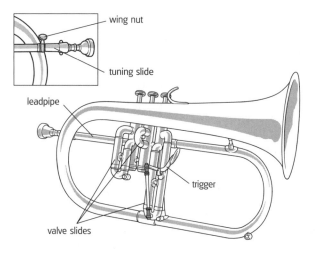

slide (the receiver) in and out of the instrument. Once the instrument is in tune, you secure the tuning slide with a wing nut.

Vertical valve slides and triggers
Tipcode TRP-005

Unlike trumpets, most flugelhorns have vertical first and third valve slides. You can't operate a vertical valve slide with a ring or a hook. That's why most flugelhorns have one or two *triggers* instead. If you pull the trigger's lever toward you, the slide will extend. Let the trigger go, and it automatically returns to its original position.

Lingo

Some lingo: Vertical slides are also known as *French style slides*. A '3rd trigger' doesn't mean there are three triggers: It's short for *third valve slide trigger*. The flugelhorn is also referred to as *fluegel* or *valved bugle*, and it's also spelled *fluegelhorn* or *flügelhorn*.

Cylindrical?

Flugelhorns are clearly conical instruments. Trumpets are often referred to as cylindrical instruments – but many parts are in fact conical. For example, many trumpets have conical leadpipes, as you can clearly see if you take a closer look. The difference in sound between flugelhorns and trumpets is mainly due to the fact that trumpets flare less than flugelhorns do: Trumpets are 'less conical.'

CORNET

There are two basic types of cornet: the American, and the British or European model. The most obvious difference is that the American cornet looks much longer. If you were to roll them both out, however, you'd see that their lengths are identical. Trumpets and flugelhorns have the same length as well.

In between

The American cornet is a little closer to the trumpet, whereas the British or *short cornet* is a little closer to the flugelhorn. You can really hear that difference. The trumpet has the most piercing sound, followed by the American cornet. The British cornet is a little mellower, and the flugelhorn has the smoothest tone. Incidentally, there are players who can make a trumpet sound almost as mellow as a flugelhorn...

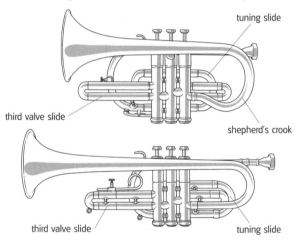

British and American-style cornets. On both models, the third valve slide sticks out some way beyond the first bend.

Shepherd's crook

The short cornet has a small extra bend, just before the bow of the bell section. This piece of tubing looks a little like the curl of a *shepherd's crook*, and that's what it's called.

The tuning slide

On most cornets, the tube has three bends between the mouthpiece and the third valve. The tuning slide is in the second bend.

Rings and hooks

Just like trumpets, many cornets have a ring on the third valve slide and a hook on the first.

TROMBONE

When people talk about trombones they usually mean the *tenor trombone.* This instrument is roughly twice as long as a trumpet. As a result, it also sounds quite a bit lower: one octave, to be precise (eight white keys on a piano).

Big mouthpiece

If you were to roll out a trombone, you'd find that it is around eight feet long. With the slide fully extended, you add nearly another three feet. It takes a pretty big mouthpiece to make the air vibrate throughout that whole length.

Two parts

The trombone consists of two main parts: the *bell section* and the *hand slide.* The two are fixed together with a *bell lock nut.* Trombonists often use the word 'bell' to refer to the entire bell section. The large bow at the back end is the tuning slide.

Inner and outer slides   Tipcode TRP-006

You operate the trombone's slide by moving the *outer slide* over the *inner slide.*

Handgrip

Your left hand holds the instrument by the *inner brace* or *handgrip,* which is attached to the inner slide. Your right hand grips the *outer brace.*

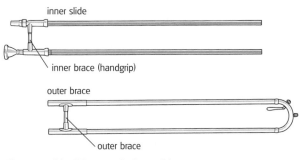

The outer slide slides over the inner slide...

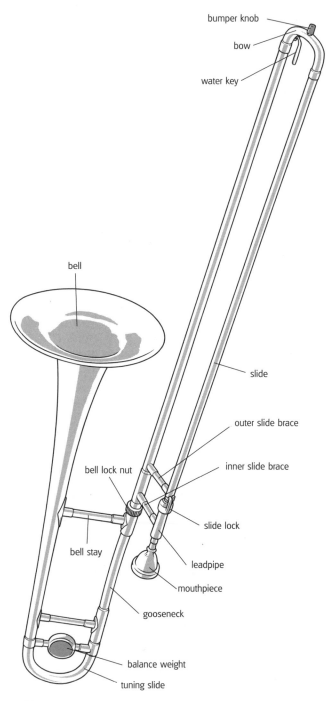

bumper knob

bow

water key

bell

slide

outer slide brace

inner slide brace

bell lock nut

slide lock

bell stay

leadpipe

mouthpiece

gooseneck

balance weight

tuning slide

Lock, knob, and water key

When you're not playing, the *slide lock* keeps the slide in place. Another security feature is the small rubber *bumper knob* on the bend of the slide, next to the water key.

Balance weight

The *bell stay* or *body brace* strengthens the bow of the bell and often has a *balance weight* or *balancer* in its center. This weight makes it a little easier to hold the instrument without it tipping forwards.

Trombones with valves

There are also trombones that have either one or two valves (see pages 50–53). A trombone with two valves is a *bass trombone*.

HOW HIGH AND HOW LOW

If you can play a trumpet or trombone well, you will have a range of around two and a half octaves or more, from the lowest note to the highest – and some players can take their instruments even higher. When you are starting out, your range will be a good deal smaller.

The same

Cornets and flugelhorns have basically the same range as a trumpet, but most players can go just a little higher on a trumpet. This is mainly due to its less conical shape.

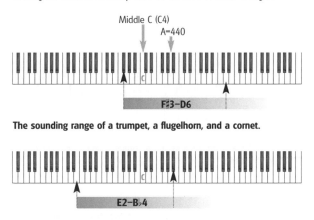

The sounding range of a trumpet, a flugelhorn, and a cornet.

The sounding range of a trombone.

15

Different pitches

If you don't use your valves, you can play a B-flat – and you can play this note at three different pitches at least: below Middle C, and one or two octaves up.

Numbers

To identify the octave in which they're played, the notes are numbered. Middle C is C4; one octave up is C5, and so on. In European literature, C4 may be indicated as c'.

IN B-FLAT

If you're a trumpeter and you see the note C in your chart, you will play that note without valves. If you would play that same pitch on a piano, you would find that what you hear is not a C, but a B-flat.

Concert B-flat...

In other words: If a trumpeter plays a C, what you hear is a *concert B-flat*. This makes a trumpet a *B-flat instrument*. Most cornets and flugelhorns are B-flat instruments too.

... C on paper

So, if a composer wants to hear one of these instruments sound a B-flat, he simply puts a C on paper. That's all there is to it.

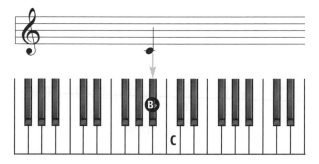

When you play a B-flat trumpet, a C on paper sounds the same as a B-flat on the piano.

Transposed chart

In a trumpet chart, a C is written down for each sounding B-flat; a D is written down if the composer wants to hear a sounding C, and so on. The chart is *transposed* to match the key of the instrument.

Transposing instrument

When you play, your trumpet transposes the music back again, so to speak. That's why a trumpet is called a *transposing instrument*. You play what your sheet music says, and your trumpet makes sure you hear what you ought to hear.

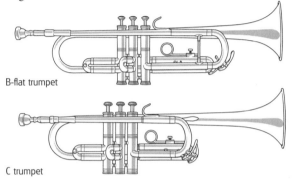

B-flat trumpet

C trumpet

The shorter C trumpet sounds brighter than the B-flat trumpet.

In G

There are also horns in other keys, and they work just the same, basically. If you have a horn in G, and the composer wants to hear a G from you, he'll write down a C. You play a C, and a G will sound.

Advantage

One major advantage of this system? No matter the key your instrument is in, each note has its own valve combination. For example, Middle C is always played without valves, regardless of the key of the instrument.

In C

Classical musicians often play the non-transposing C trumpet. Its tubing is just a little shorter than that of a B-flat instrument, which makes it sound a whole tone (whole step) higher. You can see this most clearly at the tuning slide and the third valve slide. Because it is shorter, a C trumpet sounds not only higher, but a little brighter as well. Conversely, a B-flat trumpet sounds a little darker –

and that's one of the reasons why B-flat is the most popular trumpet key.

Trombone

Trombones are B-flat instruments, just like trumpets. They're not considered transposing instruments, however. The concert B-flat you play with the slide retracted (first position) is simply notated as a B-flat.

Exception

One exception: In some types of bands this may be different, the charts showing a C if the trombones should sound a concert B-flat.

Other pitches

Trombones, trumpets, cornets, and flugelhorns come in other pitches too. There's more about them in Chapter 11, *The Family*.

Music on paper

Want to know more on transposing instruments or learn how easy it is to transpose parts? Then read *Tipbook Music on Paper – Basic Theory* (see page 134).

3. LEARNING TO PLAY

Is it hard to learn to play the trumpet or is it not that bad? Both, really. It isn't the very easiest instrument to start on, but you can play your first performances well within a year. The same is true for the other instruments in this book.

Anybody can play any note on a piano, from high to low, without knowing how to play the instrument at all. Just hit the right key. But on a brass instrument?

Make your own notes
Brass instruments don't have a key for each note. You have to make the notes yourself using just three valves, the tension of your lips, and your air stream. So learning how to play different notes will take some time.

First hear it
For one thing, you need to learn to 'hear' the note you want to play in your head, before you actually play it. If not, you'll probably play a very different note.

Which one?
You also have to learn to hear which note you're actually playing, because you can't tell by looking. That makes it like singing: You can't see which note you are singing either.

Breath control
Your lips and air stream are just as important for how you sound, and whether you're playing perfectly in tune. To be

able to play long phrases, in tune and with a good tone, you need to develop proper breath and air stream control. Playing brass instruments involves a lot more than simply blowing air into them. The first long, sustained note you play on a brass instrument will probably make you feel dizzy and light-headed. Learning how to control your breath will cure this problem.

Embouchure

You also need to develop a good *embouchure*. This French term includes just about everything you do with your lips, your tongue, and all the muscles around them ('bouche' means mouth.) You can't learn a good embouchure just like that – it takes time to build it, and then to maintain it.

Breath builders

Musicians and manufacturers have come up with various products to help you improve your air stream and your embouchure, ranging from Brass Short Cuts (a small tube with a bell, to extend your mouthpiece) to breath builders and air extenders.

LESSONS

If you take lessons, you'll learn about everything connected with playing the instrument – from breathing and embouchure to playing in tune, and from reading music to good posture.

Locating a teacher

Looking for a private teacher? Music stores may have teachers on staff, or they can refer you to one. You can also consult your local Musicians' Union, or the band director at a high school in your vicinity. Some musicians have found great teachers in performers that they caught at a concert. You may also check the classified ads in newspapers, in music magazines, or on supermarket bulletin boards, or consult the *Yellow Pages*. Professional private teachers will usually charge between twenty and fifty dollars per hour. Some make house calls, for which you'll pay extra.

Group or private lessons

Instead of taking private lessons, you can also go for group lessons, if that's an option in your vicinity. Private lessons are more expensive, but can be tailored exactly to your needs.

Collectives
You also may want to check whether there are any teacher collectives or music schools in your vicinity. These collectives may offer extras such as ensemble playing, master classes, and clinics, in a wide variety of styles and at various levels.

Questions, questions
On your first visit to a teacher, don't simply ask how much it costs. Here are some other questions.

• Is an **introductory lesson** included? This is a good way to find out how well you get on with the teacher, and, for that matter, with the instrument.
• Is the teacher interested in taking you on as a student if you are just doing it **for the fun of it**, or are you expected to practice at least three hours a day?
• Do you have to make a large investment in method books right away, or is **course material provided**?
• Are you allowed to fully concentrate on **the style of music you want to play**, or will you be required to learn other styles? Or will you be stimulated to do so?
• Is this teacher going to make you **practice scales** for two years, or will you be pushed onto a stage as soon as possible?

Trumpet, flugelhorn, or cornet...
The trumpet, flugelhorn, and cornet are all fairly similar to play. The cornet is often regarded as the easiest instrument for beginners. It is also quite small, which makes it a bit easier to hold. To play a trumpet, you need to produce more pressure, and playing a flugelhorn requires a lot of air.

Switching
Countless trumpeters also play the cornet or flugelhorn, and it is quite easy to switch from one instrument to another. If you started out on a trumpet, it's a smaller step to the cornet than to the flugelhorn (and the other way around).

Trombone

A trombone is a big instrument with a big mouthpiece, and you need a good deal of air to be able to play it. A trombone can be also difficult for small children because their arms are too short to fully extend the slide.

Smaller

This is why some teachers start children off on an alto trombone, which is a size smaller. If you switch to a tenor trombone later on, it will take some time to adjust, for instance because the slide positions are different. Other children begin on a smaller brass instrument, such as a trumpet or a cornet, or on a baritone (see page 106) and switch later to trombone.

You may start off on an alto trombone, which is a size smaller.

Other solutions

There are other solutions as well, from selecting music that doesn't require playing in the sixth or seventh positions only, to using extensions which allow even short arms to reach far enough. Also, there are trombones that have been specifically designed for junior players (page 49).

Baby teeth

If you happen to be losing your baby teeth, there's no need to stop playing, whatever brass instrument you play.

Braces

Braces may be a problem, depending on the type of braces, on the pressure you apply with the instrument, but also on your lips and the mouthpiece you use. If you do have problems, there are various commercially available lip protectors, ranging from plastic slide-on brace guards and epoxy-based solutions to lip savers that slide over your mouthpiece – and don't forget to tell your dentist you're a brass player.

PRACTICING

What goes for every instrument goes especially for wind instruments: It's better to practice half an hour every day than eight hours once a week. This is especially true for your embouchure. If you don't play for a few days, you'll feel it straight away.

Three times ten

How long should you practice? That depends on your talent and on what you want to achieve. As an indication: Half an hour a day usually results in steady progress. If playing half an hour at a stretch seems too long, try dividing it up into two quarter-hour sessions, or three of ten minutes each.

Your ear

As a horn player, you'll also need to train your ear, because it's up to you to make sure every note you play is perfectly in tune. If you play a lot, your ear will improve pretty much by itself, as will your ability to play in tune.

THE NEIGHBORS

The trumpet has for centuries been the instrument used to wake soldiers. Its potential volume has drawbacks too, however, so here are a few tips to help you practice without everyone being able to hear you.

Practice mute

A practice mute closes off the bell of your instrument. One or more tiny holes allow very little sound to come though, generally not disturbing anyone outside the room you're in. On the downside, practice mutes force you to adjust your playing: You will need to blow harder, because of the small holes, and the mute makes the pitch go up slightly – so it's often considered not a good idea to use it routinely. These mutes usually cost around forty or fifty dollars. The Peacemaker, a special practice mute with plastic tubes and earplugs, costs about the same.

A practice mute.

Silent Brass

The Yamaha Silent Brass costs about six times as much, but it goes a step further. The system consists of a plastic mute with a built-in microphone, a small amplifier, and a pair of headphones. The amp has an input for a cassette or CD player, so you can silently play along with prerecorded music. You can also hook up a second Silent Brass, or a home keyboard, for instance. A built-in reverb adds some space and life to the sound.

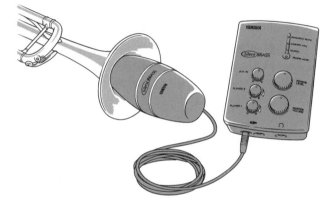

Practice mute with built-in microphone and amplifier (Yamaha).

Fixed practice times

If you want to play without a practice mute, and neighbors or housemates are bothered by your playing, it may be enough to simply agree to fixed practice times. If you really play a lot, it may be better to insulate a room. Even a very large cupboard can be big enough. There are books available on sound insulation, or you can hire a specialized contractor. Of course, it may be easier to find a place that works a little better for practicing.

Your own ears

If you play in a small room or with a loud band, think about protecting your ears. The most basic ear plugs make it difficult to play, because they simply stop up your ears. More expensive protectors usually don't make your instrument (or the band) sound as if it were in another room. The best – and most expensive – solution is often a set of custom-made ear protectors with adjustable filters.

On CD

Most music is supposed to be played in a group, so it's often more fun to practice 'together' too – even if there aren't any other musicians around. There are all kinds of CDs available to play along to, in all kinds of styles, for beginners as well as for more advanced brass players. Your own part is left off, leaving the other musicians for you to play with.

Computer lessons

If you have a computer handy, you can also practice with special CD-ROMs. Some feature entire orchestras: You can decide for yourself how fast you want a piece to be played, and which parts you want to hear. Some software allows you to slow down difficult phrases on a recording, so you can find out what's going on at your own tempo.

Metronome

Most pieces of music are supposed to be played just as fast at the end as at the beginning. Playing with a metronome helps you to achieve this. A metronome is a small mechanical or electronic device that ticks or bleeps out a steady adjustable pulse, so you can tell immediately if you're dragging or speeding.

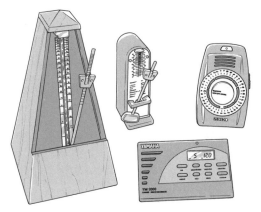

Two mechanical metronomes and two electronic ones.

Recording

If you record your lessons, you can listen to what was said, and especially how you sounded, when you get home. You can learn a lot by listening carefully to yourself playing. That's why many musicians record themselves when they are practicing. All you need is a cassette recorder with a built-in microphone. Better equipment (a minidisc recorder with a separate microphone, for instance) is more expensive but yields more informative and enjoyable results.

Listen and play

And finally, visit festivals, concerts, and sessions. Watch and listen to orchestras, concert bands, and other groups. One of the best ways to learn to play is through seeing other musicians at work. Living legends or local amateurs – every concert's a learning experience. And the best way to learn to play? Play a lot!

4. BUYING BRASS

Because they are not all that complicated, you can buy a decent trumpet, trombone, flugelhorn or cornet at an affordable price. This chapter will give you an idea of what everything costs and the best places to go to buy an instrument, new or secondhand. Chapter 5 has tips on choosing and play-testing instruments.

Brass instruments are quite affordable. You can get a brand new trumpet for as little as two or three hundred dollars, and that includes a mouthpiece and a case. A reliable, good-sounding intermediate instrument that you can enjoy for many years, will set you back some four to eight hundred dollars or more. The same goes for flugelhorns, cornets, and trombones, with the exception that the cheapest models of those instruments will usually cost a little more.

Pro instruments
Instruments with a 'professional' label start around fifteen hundred to two thousand dollars. Want to spend more? There are plenty of instruments that cost three, four or five thousand dollars, and the most expensive models on the market will set you back well over fifteen grand.

Looking and playing
Professional brasswind instruments look pretty much the same as the very cheapest models. To *see* the differences you need to take a close look. To *hear* the differences you need to be a fairly experienced player. Here are some of those differences.

CHAPTER 4

More time

Compared to student models, more time and care is devoted to making more expensive instruments. As a result, they sound better and last longer. More work is done by hand, from hammering the bell to hand-lapping the pistons and the slides, aiming for an airtight seal and smooth operation.

More expensive materials

For a higher price you may also get better brass, a bell made of a special alloy, or a silver-plated or even gold-plated instrument. Better materials may also allow for easier repairs.

More choice

The more you spend, the more choice you usually have. More expensive instruments may come with a selection of different leadpipes, tuning slides or bells, for instance, so that you can tailor the instrument to your preferences. There are brands which offer one single type of trumpet in fifty variations...

Better not

The quality of budget instruments can be quite amazing, offering good sound and playability for a very reasonable price. Nevertheless, you may come across cheap instruments you'd better not buy – because they'll never really play in tune or sound good, or because the pistons don't move as easily as they should or don't provide an airtight seal for an extended period of time.

Another player

To hear how good an instrument is, you need to be able to play quite well. That's unlikely to be the case if you're buying your first one. So take someone with you who can play, or go to a shop with versatile brass players on staff.

BUYING NEW, SECONDHAND, OR ONLINE

You're always best off buying your instrument in a store whose employees really know what they're talking about. Then you can be virtually certain that you'll end up with a good instrument, matching your playing level, style, personal taste, and budget.

Fast repairs

If you buy it in a shop that does its own repairs, you will usually get your instrument back quickly if anything does go wrong with it.

Privately or in a store

Secondhand instruments are sold through music stores, or they're offered for sale in the classified sections in newspapers, on bulletin boards in stores, and on the Internet. If you buy an instrument through an ad, you may pay less than in a store. After all, the store owner needs to make a living too.

In a music store

All the same, buying from a music store does have advantages. The instrument may have been checked and adjusted, and it may come with a warranty; you can go back if you have any questions; and you may be able to choose between a number of instruments. Another advantage: A reputable store will never charge you much more than an instrument is worth. A private seller might, either because he doesn't know better or because he thinks you don't.

A second opinion

If you go to buy a secondhand horn, it's even more important to take along an advanced player who knows about the instrument – especially if you're going to buy privately. Otherwise you might turn down a decent horn just because it doesn't look good, or get saddled with one that looks great but doesn't sound good or play in tune. Some technical tips for buying secondhand instruments begin on page 56.

Appraisal

If you want to be sure you're not paying too much, get the instrument appraised first. A good store or workshop can tell you exactly what it's worth, whether it needs any work done, and what that'll cost.

Buying online

You can also buy musical instruments online or by mail-order. This makes it impossible to compare instruments. Online and mail-order companies usually do offer a return service for most or all of their products: If you're not happy with your purchase, you can send it back within a certain period of time. Of course the instrument should be in new condition when you return it.

RENTING

If you're not sure whether you want to play the horn, you can rent one first, starting at some ten to twenty dollars per month. The exact rental fee, usually a percentage of the retail price of the instrument, will also depend on what it covers – *i.e.*, do you rent a new or a used (rental-return) instrument, and are insurance and repairs included? Some stores may ask for a deposit; others may require your credit card number.

... and then buying

Some stores offer a rent-to-own program, where all or part of the rental fee you've been paying will be deducted if you decide to buy the instrument in the end. Alternatively, you may get a discount on a new instrument, after the rental period: The longer you've been renting, the larger the discount will be. These are just two of the many variations you may come across.

AND FINALLY

What you consider the best trumpet may well be the one your favorite horn player has. Does that mean you should buy one like it? There isn't much point. One and the same musician will sound pretty much the same on two different instruments – but two different musicians on the same horn won't sound the same at all. In other words: The sound is determined mainly by the player rather than the instrument.

More information

If you want to be well informed before you go out to get an instrument, new or secondhand, get hold of as many brasswind brochures and catalogs as you can find, along with the price lists.

Various magazines offer reviews and other articles on the instrument. Quite a few brasswind books are available too, as well as loads of information on the Internet. You'll find titles, addresses, and other information beginning on page 127.

Fairs

One last tip: If a music trade fair or brasswind convention is being held anywhere near you, go and check it out. Besides being able to try and compare a considerable number of instruments, you will also have the chance to meet plenty of product specialists, as well as numerous fellow horn players who can provide information and inspiration.

5. A GOOD INSTRUMENT

You can get lacquered, silver-plated, and even gold-plated horns. Instruments with different bells and different bores, with rings or triggers, or with special tuning slides, and so on. This chapter tells you all about those differences and how they do or don't influence the sound of the instrument, or its playability.

Play-testing tips and how to compare instruments by ear are covered in this chapter too, as well as tips for buying secondhand instruments.

The first and longest section of this chapter is about the different parts of the instruments and how they affect their sound and playability. If you prefer to choose an instrument using your ears only, then go straight to the tips on page 53 and onwards.

Lacquer

Bare, untreated brass makes your hands smell, and it tarnishes very easily. That's why brass instruments are usually finished with a high-gloss (epoxy) lacquer, which is either clear or one with a very slight golden hue. Matte-finished horns are also available.

Silver-plated

Silver-plated instruments are more expensive, and you have to polish them more often, but the plating lasts longer than lacquer. A silver-plated trumpet will soon cost seventy-five to a hundred dollars more than an identical lacquered instrument. Of course, not all instruments are available in both finishes.

Sound

A lacquer coating is much thicker than a silver plating, which is why lacquered instruments are often said to sound a little warmer, smoother, mellower, or less bright: The lacquer finish reportedly mutes the sound ever so slightly. Most musicians can't tell the difference in blindfold tests, though. In fact, the difference between two 'identical' trumpets with the same finish may easily be bigger.

Gold-plated

There are several gold-plated instruments around too. The extra money buys you a sound which can be described, again, as a little 'richer.' Of course, if only the valve caps are gold-plated, or the inside of the bell, you are unlikely to hear the difference.

Nickel-plated

Nickel-plated trumpets, which are said to sound a little shallower and less expressive, are rare nowadays. Some parts are still nickel-plated, though. Nickel looks different than silver: It has a slightly 'harder' shine. Some other differences are that it costs less, and it is easier to maintain. Nickel lasts at least as long as silver. Its main drawback is that many people are allergic to it.

Different looks

Sometimes you'll see three types of metal on one horn: a yellow brass instrument with a gold brass bell and nickel-plated slides, for instance. Colored instruments, available in black, red, blue, and other colors, are popular mainly in the US.

Trim

The instrument's *trim* includes the bottom and top valve caps, valve stems, water keys, finger buttons, and other replaceable parts. Some brands offer trim kits, which allow you to enhance the looks of your horn with gold-plated parts, for example.

Raw brass

Contrary to what you might think, unfinished instruments that show raw, unpolished brass, are usually handmade and very expensive.

BELL MATERIAL

Quite often, the bell will be a slightly different color to the rest of the instrument, indicating that a different material has been used – brass containing more copper, for instance. This does more than enhancing the looks of the instrument; it influences the sound as well. On more expensive instruments you can often choose from a variety of bells.

Darker, warmer, and redder

The more copper the brass contains, the darker and warmer the sound usually becomes, and the redder the color. Some musicians also find that the extra copper makes the instrument respond a little faster.

Gold brass and red brass

The type of brass used for most brass instruments contains around seventy percent copper. It's often called *yellow brass*. There are several names for brass with extra copper. One brand calls it *gold brass*, another *rose brass*; alloys with an especially high copper content are usually referred to as *red brass*. Whether you pay more for extra copper depends on the brand.

Silver, bronze, or glass

There are also bells made of other materials. For instance, a bell made of solid silver or bronze supposedly gives you a much brighter sound, and there are even trumpets with bells made of glass, for instance.

Engraved

The brand name is almost always engraved into the bell. You may find ornamental engraving there too, which could raise the price of the horn some fifty to five hundred dollars or more. Some brands offer a choice of patterns.

THE BORE

If you pinch the end of a garden hose, you get a hard, fierce jet of water. Wind instruments work in much the same way. The narrower a tube is, the 'fiercer' or edgier the sound becomes. The inside diameter of the tube is known as the *bore*.

Diameter

Catalogs often tell you the size of an instrument's bore, which is usually measured at the second valve slide. On a trumpet, a large bore would be 0.462" or more; a small bore is about 0.455" or less. When you play, you'll know that these differences are much bigger than they may look on paper…

Medium-large

In order to play a trumpet with a large bore, you need a good embouchure and good breath control. A very small bore requires an experienced player too. Most trumpets have a bore size of about 0.460" (11.68 mm). This medium-large bore is a good choice for beginners as well.

Larger bore

A larger bore helps you to create a larger sound: bigger, more open and broad, and also a little mellower, warmer, and darker. The larger bore also makes for a free-blowing horn with plenty of volume, though it's trickier to play very softly. It's also slightly easier to influence the tone or *timbre* of the instrument, as well as its pitch – and the later can make it harder to play in tune.

Large-bore horns tend to blend very well with other instruments. Together with the other characteristics, this explains why large-bore instruments are often used in symphony orchestras.

Smaller bore

Trumpets with a smaller bore are rare. Basically, a smaller bore gives a brighter, lighter, edgier sound. You can do less to influence the tone – it's harder to color the sound – but it's also easier to play in tune, as you can't influence pitch as much as with a larger bore. Low notes are harder to play. A smaller bore may give you less volume, but the sound will often project better – which is why it doesn't blend as easily.

How big?

Some manufacturers indicate the bore size with figures; others use words like small, medium, and large. Should the bore size be given in millimeters, divide by 25.4 to get inches (*i.e.*, 11.73mm ÷ 25.4 = 0.462").

Trombone bores

Trombonists often start on an instrument with a relatively small bore, usually 0.485" or 0.490". A large-bore instrument (0.547") requires more air support than a beginning player will be able to supply. Bass trombones are a little wider still (0.562" to 0.578").

Dual-bore trombones...

On trombones with a *dual bore*, the first inner tube of the slide (*upper slide tube*) is less wide than the second (*lower slide tube*). A popular combination is 0.525"/0.547". The narrower upper tube makes the instrument play like a smaller-bore horn, while the wider lower tube gives you the bigger sound of a wider bore instrument. The increasing bore, from tube to tube, also makes the instrument a little more 'conical.' This results in a warmer, mellower sound. Dual-bore trombones are sometimes used as an in-between step to a larger-bore instrument. Another part where the bore may vary is the first piece of tubing of the bell section, known as the *gooseneck* (see page 49). Some companies offer goosenecks with a selection of different bore sizes.

... and trumpets

There are dual-bore trumpets too, which are smaller on the top of the main tuning slide, and wider at the valve section. This increasing diameter has the same effect as a conical bore, so – again – it makes for a warmer, darker sound.

Shape

Two instruments that have the same bore size may nonetheless sound and play very differently. Why? For one thing, the bore size only indicates the diameter of the tube at a certain point. The sound of the instrument, however, is influenced by the bore of the entire instrument – the way the tubing widens from the start of the mouthpiece receiver to the bell's rim. The different tapers or flarings aren't always easy to see – but you can easily hear them, and you can feel them too, when you play.

Less conical

An example would be that American-made flugelhorns often sound a little brighter than European models, because the American models are less conical: They often start a little wider, and they're less wide at the bell.

THE BELL

Both the bell size and the flare of the bell have an influence on the sound, as well as on how freely the horn blows.

How big

The bell of a trumpet or cornet is usually no bigger than 5" (12.7 cm) in diameter. Flugelhorn bells usually range from 6" to 6.75". Tenor trombone bells may range from 7" to 9", and many bass trombones come with a 10" bell. To preserve the round shape and to protect the edge, most bells have a *wire reinforced rim*.

Taper

Some bells flare only toward the very end of the instrument (slow taper). On other models the flare begins sooner. This latter is known as a gradual taper or, contradictory as it may sound, a fast taper. The more gradual the taper, the more the bell will behave like a large one, making for a warmer and darker tone, a bigger sound, and easier low notes. A less gradual taper will make for a more controllable, brighter-sounding instrument, just like a smaller bell – or an instrument with a smaller bore.

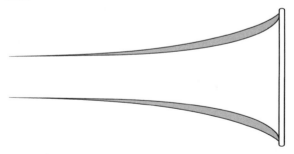

If you include the gray sections, you'll see a gradual taper.

Six bells

In their professional series, some brands offer six or more different bells, each with a different taper, for the same trumpet.

One-piece bells

Most more expensive instruments have a one-piece bell, made of a single sheet of brass (see Chapter 12). A two-piece bell is cheaper to make, but a one-piece bell is said to make for a brighter-sounding, more responsive instrument and a better projection. One-piece bells are also referred to as *solid* or *seamless bells*.

Tuning with your bell

Some expensive trumpets can be tuned with the bell. This *tuning bell* or *tunable bell* can be extended at the bell tail, just beyond the third valve. Supporters of tunable bells say they give you a better tone: Getting rid of the tuning slide (or being able to leave it all the way in) enhances a smoother air flow in the instrument. It reduces the turbulence, so to speak. Critics say instruments with tuning bells don't tune properly. To keep everybody happy there are trumpets with both a tunable bell and a tuning slide.

Different bells

If you can tune with the bell, you can also change bells, and use a red brass one if you need a warmer sound, and a solid silver one for lead playing, for instance. A tuning bell doesn't allow for fixed braces between the bell and the leadpipe, making the instrument more vulnerable.

The sound of the bell

You sometimes see horn players flicking a fingernail against the bell to hear what sound it makes. Some say you can tell a lot about how the whole instrument sounds this way. Others disagree, stating that there are awful horns with great-sounding bells, and just as many fine instruments with bells that don't sound good at all.

Upbell

If you like the looks, you can also get yourself an instrument with an upturned bell, known as an *upbell*, such as the instrument that the late jazz trumpeter Dizzy Gillespie always played. Reportedly, the design was created by accident when somebody fell or stepped on Gillespie's instrument, bending the bell upwards as he did. Gillespie commented that he could hear himself better with the bell at an upward angle.

THE LEADPIPE

You hear less about leadpipes than about bells, mainly because the differences are smaller – so small, in fact, that you can barely see them. But they're there. That's why some instruments come with interchangeable leadpipes, which feature different tapers and materials (*i.e.*, brass, nickel, or silver).

Flare

Like bells, leadpipes may have slower or faster tapers. A more gradual taper will yield a warmer sound, and vice versa. Also, leadpipes may have larger or smaller bores, with the same effect as the bore size of the entire instrument. Some brands offer special *multi-tapered leadpipes* or step-bore designs, their exact effect depending on their dimensions.

Three choices

On some trumpets you can choose from two, three, or more different leadpipes. You do need to make that choice in advance, because you can't change them yourself. On trombones you usually can.

Material

The leadpipe's material is not of the greatest importance to the sound, but it does affect how long the leadpipe will last. For example, brass with a higher copper content (*i.e.*, rose brass or gold brass) is less susceptible to the corrosive effect of saliva.

Reversed leadpipe

The smoother the path from the mouthpiece to the bell, the smoother the tone can be. That's why many instruments have a *reversed leadpipe*: The tuning slide doesn't slide into the leadpipe, but over it. As a result, the vibrating air column in the instrument is not disturbed by the small step at the beginning of the tuning slide. The same solution is referred to as a *reversed tuning slide* –– which actually is a more accurate name.

Easier to play

Trumpets with reversed leadpipes are said to be easier to play, or to play in tune. Other players prefer to have that bit more blowing resistance, or they simply prefer playing with a 'regular' instrument for any other reason. Trumpets with a reversed leadpipe are available in just about all price ranges. In some series it's offered as an option.

TUNING SLIDE

Tuning slides come in two basic models. One is a little rounder; the other a little more angular. Some expensive trumpets come with one of each.

Single-radius, dual-radius

The round model is called a *single-radius tuning slide*; the model with the angular crook is referred to as a *dual-radius* or *square-bend tuning slide*, among other names. Most players consider the round model easier to play, and say it sounds 'rounder', just as it looks rounder. With the angular design, the instrument supposedly responds a little better, and high notes are easier to hit. Of course, not everyone agrees – if only because not everyone tries the same slides on the same trumpets…

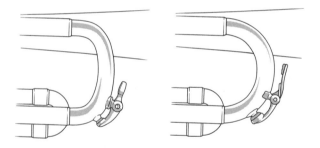

A dual-radius and a single-radius tuning slide.

Braces and sound

Some tuning slides have one or even two reinforcing braces. The added weight also contributes to the sound (see page 42).

Trombones

The bend at the end of a trombone slide can also be angular or rounded. The shape does have less effect on the sound than that of a trumpet's tuning slide.

WATER KEYS

Most water keys are very basic, reliable 'see-saw' keys with a spring and a small cork, but there are some small variations. For example, the cork can be replaced by a rubber insert shaped to fill the hole of the water key – again, to reduce the turbulence in the instrument.

Amado

Other manufacturers prefer to use the Amado water key. It's less prone to leakage, as it has no cork, and its looks are quite modest, compared to a traditional water key. Also, they're said to reduce the instrument's playing resistance.

An Amado water key.

First-valve water key only

Some instruments have a first-valve water key only. On cheap instruments that's just to save money. When an expensive instrument has no third valve water key, it's usually said to improve the sound and intonation of the instrument. Either way, you have to remove the third slide (or a separate crook on that slide) to get rid of the moisture.

HEAVY OR LIGHT

Not all horns weigh the same. Light-weight trumpets, for example, have a somewhat 'lighter' and livelier sound, and they are lighter to play and have a quicker response than heavy-weight models, which makes them sought after by many jazz or Latin musicians. Weight differences can be traced back mainly to the wall thickness of the tubing – but there are other ways to make an instrument heavier too.

Heavier

Heavy-weight instruments tend to have a 'heavier', thicker, richer, darker, and more focused tone than thin-wall versions. They allow you to play high notes at high volumes without the sound distorting or getting edgy or metallic. On the other hand, the heavier an instrument is, the harder work it is to play it.

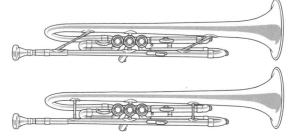

The braces between leadpipe and bell may be straight or diagonal.

Braces

Rather than using heavier tubing, extra mass can be supplied by adding parts to the instrument. Some instruments have double leadpipes (twin tubes), or extra heavy finger hooks and rings, for instance, but adding braces or using diagonal braces (which need to be longer) helps as well.

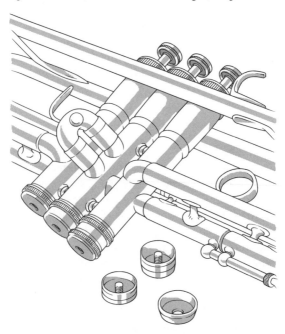

Trumpet with interchangeable bottom caps (Conn).

Heavy caps

You can add weight yourself too. One example would be to fit your instrument with extra-heavy (weighted) *bottom valve caps*, available in different sizes and weights. Some instruments are supplied with a complete set. Similar and alternative add-on weights are available for other horns as well. Conversely, some trombones have a removable balance weight – but that has more effect on the balance than on the sound of the instrument.

Heavy all over

Monette, Courtois, and a few other brands make extremely heavy, expensive trumpets, that weigh nearly twice as much as normal instruments, with double-wall bells, heavy-wall tubing, and other special features.

An extra-heavy trumpet with a double-wall bell, centering sound plates, and other features (Courtois Evolution).

Mouthpieces

Adding mass to your mouthpiece has a similar effect, as you can read on pages 71–72.

VALVE SLIDES

On most trumpets and cornets you can fine-tune certain notes with the first and third valve slides. On most flugelhorns, only the third valve slide is adjustable. If you're a trombone player, you may want to skip the following section, and move on to page 48.

Too high

Trumpets, cornets, and flugelhorns all have a few notes that normally sound a little *sharp* (too high). You can lower those notes by moving the third valve slide out a little. Why not simply make that tube a little longer? Because that would make other notes sound *flat* (too low).

Ring

An adjustable third valve slide ring can be set to accommodate shorter (children's) fingers. It's usually found on student instruments only.

Security

If you move the third slide out too far, it can slip off the instrument. A *slide stop* prevents that. Some slide stops are adjustable, so you can set the distance the slide is allowed to travel.

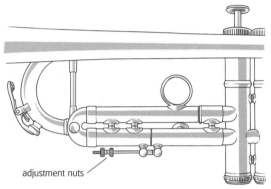

adjustment nuts

A third valve slide with an adjustable slide stop.

First valve slide

Many instruments have either a ring or a hook on the first valve slide as well, and on some instruments it's an option.

Lipping up

Some players think you shouldn't use the first valve slide at all: First valve notes should be adjusted with your embouchure only ('lipping up' or 'lipping down'). Don't worry about all this if you just started playing: You usually get into fine-tuning only after a couple of years.

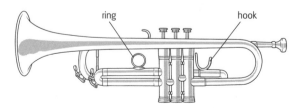

ring   hook

A ring on the third valve slide; a hook or saddle on the first.

Second valve slide

The second slide, short as it is, isn't used for fine-tuning. It usually has a small button or *pull* that makes it easier to take it off for cleaning purposes.

Flugelhorns

Because of its conical shape, the pitch of a flugelhorn is easier to adjust with your embouchure – which is why many flugelhorns come without adjustable slides. If one slide only is adjustable, it's the longest one: the third, which has most influence on the pitch.

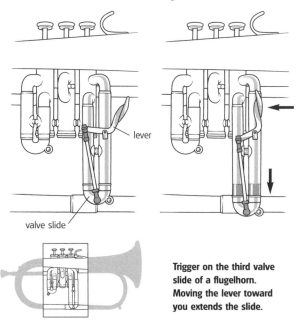

Trigger on the third valve slide of a flugelhorn. Moving the lever toward you extends the slide.

Triggers on trumpets

Some trumpeters prefer a trigger to the traditional ring or a hook – especially on the first slide, because this one is a little harder to shift with your thumb. If you can choose, getting an instrument with a trigger can easily cost an additional hundred fifty dollars. Confusing: Some call a regular valve slide a 'trigger' too – but it isn't really one.

Nickel silver and brass

To make slides slide as smoothly as they should, various alloys and combinations are used. A popular combination is nickel silver for the inside tubes, and brass for the outer tubes. Nickel silver is also used for mouthpiece receivers: The alloy helps to prevent your mouthpiece from getting stuck.

Additional slides

Some instruments come with one or more extra valve slides or tuning slides, which allows them to be used in more than one key: For example, using slightly longer slides, you can turn a C trumpet into a B-flat instrument (see also page 102).

PISTON VALVES

Most trumpets, cornets and flugelhorns have piston valves, in which a piston moves up and down. This piston is a tube through which three tubular holes (*ports* or *portholes*) run diagonally.

Up and down   Tipcode TRP-007

If a valve is in the 'up' position, the air will take the shortest possible path, straight through port number one. If you depress the valve, the air will be diverted through the second porthole, around the valve slide and back out through the third port. Want to see how it works? Remove the second valve slide, and take a look inside while depressing the second valve.

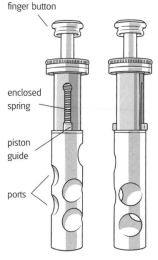

finger button

Top or bottom

In the past, piston valves were usually *bottom-sprung*: The spring which brings the valve back up was below the piston, at the bottom of the valve casing. Most modern instruments are *top-sprung*. This *top-action* design usually has enclosed springs, so they won't jump out when you remove the pistons. Today,

enclosed spring

piston guide

ports

Top-sprung piston valve.

bottom-sprung or *bottom-action* valves are found mainly on flugelhorns and old or low-budget trumpets.

Monel

Most instruments have pistons made of *monel*, an alloy which slides well and doesn't wear easily. Alternatively, some (usually expensive) instruments come with stainless steel pistons, for instance, which are said to be very durable. If the alloy of an instrument isn't specified, it's usually a beginners' model that features a cheaper metal.

Piston guide

Piston guides, also known as *valve guides*, make sure that the piston's ports always align with the tubing, to prevent them from rotating in their casings. There are one- and two-point, metal and non-metal piston guides. You may come across every possible variation in most price ranges.

Smooth

When checking out an instrument, try the pistons for smooth, silent, and quick action. Of course they should be lubricated to function properly. If you depress a valve and then slide your finger off of the finger button, it shouldn't rattle or rebound.

Breaking them in

Often, the pistons start to slide as smoothly as they should only once the instrument has been played for a while: They need to be 'broken in', just like the engine of a new car.

Springs

Naturally, not all valve springs are the same. If springs feel too stiff or too light, you can have them replaced quite cheaply. Some players reduce the springiness of their springs by making them shorter – but buying shorter or less springy springs allows you to switch back too.

Finger buttons

Finger buttons come in different weights and shapes. Some players prefer concave buttons, for instance. If you're looking for a lighter, quicker action, you may get a set of light-weight finger buttons. Want something special? There are finger buttons with precious gem inlays too.

Skip the trombone

If you want to skip the trombone section, go ahead to page 53 and beyond.

TROMBONES

Trombones are different from trumpets because they have a slide, for one thing. Some have valves too, but they're different from a trumpet's valves. First, a closer look at the slide.

Stockings

If you take a close look at the ends of the inner slide of a trombone, you'll see a small bulge on either tube. The outer slide moves over these *stockings* rather than sliding over the entire inner slide – which makes it go a lot smoother.

Materials

The inner slide is often made of a different material than the outer slide – nickel silver on the inside, brass on the outside, for instance. This makes the slide action as smooth possible, and it prevents corrosion. Another way to enhance the slide's action is through using seamless tubing, which can be found only in more expensive instruments.

Light-weight slide

On some trombones you can opt for a *light-weight slide.* This will make the instrument 'feel' a little lighter and respond a little more easily. In the same vein, a few brands offer a *narrow slide*, which is a little lighter to play.

Different slide

If a trombone sounds good but doesn't slide smoothly, try replacing the slide with one from an identical instrument.

Barrels

The *receiver barrels*, into which the hand slide falls, have a cork washer or a spring inside. Spring-loaded barrels allow you to pull the slide toward you a little further in the first position, and some trombonists use that difference to make certain notes sound a little higher.

Curve

The slight curve halfway along the gooseneck makes the slide point downwards a little. This improves the balance of the instrument.

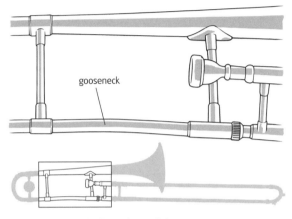

gooseneck

The gooseneck nearly always has a slight curve.

Junior trombone

There are also trombones with a much larger arching in the gooseneck. This makes it fit more comfortably around your neck, and it slightly reduces the overall length of the instrument. The first trombone of this kind, designed especially with children in mind, also has a shorter slide than a regular trombone, as well as a special pistol grip and an adjustable thumb rest.

Ring

A simple solution for smaller hands is a ring on the inner slide brace. You put your first finger through the ring, instead of resting it against the mouthpiece or the receiver.

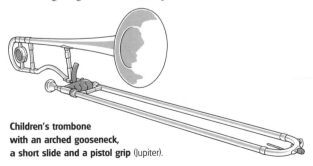

**Children's trombone
with an arched gooseneck,
a short slide and a pistol grip** (Jupiter).

F-attachment

A trombone plays an octave lower than a trumpet, basically. There are trombones that can go a little lower still, with an extra piece of tubing and a valve. With this extra length, the B-flat in the first position (the *pedal note*) becomes an F, hence the name *F-attachment* for the extra tubing and valve together.

Rotary valve

The valve of the F-attachment is a *rotary valve*, which is slightly more complicated than a piston valve. Rotary valves are also known as *rotors* or *cylinder valves*.

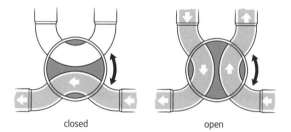

closed   open

A rotary valve.

Other positions

An F-attachment not only allows you to play lower notes: You can also play many of the original notes in new positions, which makes certain trills and phrases easier, for instance. The price difference between a trombone without and with an F-attachment can easily vary from one to four hundred dollars, depending – among other things – on the price and the brand of the instrument.

Open or traditional

The extra tubing which goes with an F-attachment can either stick out some way behind the tuning slide, or be

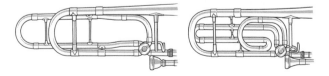

Trombones with F-attachments: an open wrap on the left and a traditional one on the right.

compactly curled up inside the main tube. The first solution is known as an *open wrap*; the second is a *traditional* or *closed wrap*.

Free blowing but vulnerable
An open wrap avoids sharp bends in the tubing. This makes for a more free-blowing instrument, and reduces the difference between playing with the F-attachment or 'open' (*i.e.*, without F-attachment). On the other hand, an open wrap is more vulnerable, as the tubing sticks out. There are all kinds of in-between wrap designs as well.

Convertible and straight trombones
On a *convertible trombone* you can take the whole F-attachment (*F-section, F-wrap*) off if you don't need it. Trombones without an F-attachment are referred to as *straight trombones*.

Bass trombone
A bass trombone is basically the same size as a tenor trombone, but it has a larger bore and bell, which makes the very lowest notes easier to play. Another difference is that nearly all bass trombones have two valves. The second one adds another piece of tubing to the instrument, so you can go down to E-flat or D.

In-line or offset
On most older bass trombones, you can't use the second valve without the first one. This system is known as *stacked* or *offset*. The newer *in-line* or *independent* system, developed in the late 1960s, allows you to use both valves independently.

Not the same
That second rotor doesn't do the same thing on all bass trombones. It usually puts the instrument in the key of G-flat or G. Using both valves or rotors will then allow you to play low E-flat or D respectively.

Interchangeable tubing
Some bass trombones have interchangeable tubes for the second rotor, so that you can adapt its effect to the key you play in, for instance.

Valve linkages: string or metal

There are two basic types of trombone valve linkages. *Mechanical* or *ball-and-socket linkages* use metal parts only. The other type uses a nylon string, with names like *string rotor action*, *string action*, or string *F-valve linkage*.

A string is cheaper and more likely to be noiseless; it also has a shorter lever stroke, and it's fairly easy to adjust yourself. On the other hand, strings can break or come loose.

Feel...

A good, properly adjusted mechanism with a mechanical linkage is more expensive, and can be just as quiet. Of course, if one trombonist says a string 'feels' better, the next will disagree. Depending on the brand, you may be able to choose between string or metal. Conversion kits (mechanical to string) are also available.

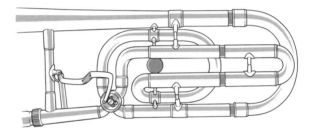

An F-attachment with a string action.

Testing

If you are play-testing a trombone with rotors, feel how smoothly the rotors work, listen to make sure they don't rattle when you let go of the lever, check the lever stroke, see if it's adjustable, and compare how the trombone plays with and without rotors. Using the rotor(s) usually increases the blowing resistance of the instrument, and the tone may be slightly altered. The exact effect may vary from one instrument to the other.

With or without rotors

A trombone usually plays differently as soon as you use the rotor: Not only are you adding a fair length of tubing, but the air also needs to travel around lots of extra bends, especially the tight bends in the rotor itself.

New designs

In order to reduce this difference, all kinds of new valves have been devised. Two well-known names are Thayer, Hagmann, Rotax (Willson), and CL2000 (Conn). Some brands offer a choice between these new designs and traditional rotors. Retrofitting your instrument with a modern valve easily costs close to a thousand dollars.

Valved trombone

A *valved trombone* is something quite different again: It has the same piston valves as a trumpet, and no slide. Most brands have only one model in their catalogs. As the fingering is familiar and you don't need to get used to a hand slide, a valved trombone is a popular choice for trumpeters who want to be able to play trombone as well. Jazz players are the most likely to do so, hence the alternative name *jazz trombone*.

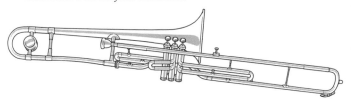

A valved trombone with three piston valves, and no slide.

IN TUNE

On every wind instrument, there are notes that tend to sound sharp or flat. On trumpets, cornets, and flugelhorns, for example, you will need to adjust most of the notes that you play with the first and third slide combined (*e.g.*, low G and low D tend to be sharp; high F tends to be flat; and so on). You adjust these pitches with the adjustable valve slide(s), with your embouchure, or both.

Intonation

Usually, the better an instrument, the less you have to adjust these pitches. The lingo: Better instruments usually have better *intonation*.

The wrong side

Every designer has his own ideas about how to improve the intonation of an instrument. As a result, every horn has its own deviations. If you are used to having to adjust a certain note on your trumpet, and you do the same on a new instrument, that note may suddenly sound off – because the new trumpet has better intonation, so you are overcompensating. In other words: You'll need to get used to a different horn, especially if the intonation is different.

Tests
There are a few tests you can do to hear how good the intonation of an instrument is, assuming you can play. If you hear deviations even without using the valves, it's probably better to put it away. Next, play all the notes you can get with the first valve, then with the second, and so on. Another test: Play the scale of B, as this contains quite a lot of potential off-notes.

Trombone
Of course, a trombone is different, as the hand slide allows you to fine-tune every single note. So is there such a thing as an out-of-tune trombone? Yes: A trombone has bad intonation if the positions are too far from where they should be. When trying out a trombone pay special attention to middle and high F, middle D and high B-flat, which can be flat. High notes are more likely to be out of tune than low ones, and you're more likely to hear that they are out of tune too.

GOOD SOUND
Of course, an instrument not only needs good intonation, it also needs to have a good sound, whatever 'good' means. If you don't yet play or you haven't been playing very long, you should ask a decent player to help you go through the following tips.

Somebody else
If you get somebody else to play a horn for you, it will never sound the same as when you play that instrument yourself. But as long as the same person demonstrates a number of horns for you, you will still be able to hear the differences between the instruments. Getting someone else to play also allows you to hear what they sound like at a distance – which is what your audience will hear.

Your mouthpiece

When choosing an instrument, always use your own mouthpiece, or an identical one. Otherwise you won't be listening to the differences between the instruments you're playing, but to how you sound with one or more different mouthpieces.

The wall

As wind instruments direct the sound away from you, it's hard to get an idea of what your audience will hear. A tip: Play facing a wall, so the sound is reflected back to you. Trombonists can't use the slide that way. A solution? Put a book on a music stand and point the bell at the book.

Briefly at first

If you have to choose between a whole load of instruments, it's often best if you play only briefly on each one. Play something simple, so that you can concentrate on the instrument's tone, rather then on the notes you're playing.

Two by two

Once you have made a basic selection this way, start comparing the instruments two by two or three by three. Replace the one you like least with one from you basic selection. Compare. Replace the one you like least. And so on. Once you're about to make your final decision, you may want to play longer pieces so that you get to know the instruments better.

Mellow or bright

If you have no idea where to start when you walk into a store, ask the salesperson for two very different-sounding instruments – one with a very mellow character, and another that's known for its bright sound, for instance. Decide which sound you prefer and go on from there. Or try a very cheap one alongside the most expensive one they have, just to hear how much they differ.

Response

An instrument must have a good response: Notes must speak easily and consistently. Try the response with loud and soft notes, from high to low. If you can hear the softest notes at the back of the hall, the horn has good projection.

Loud or soft

An instrument doesn't just sound louder when you play harder; it sounds different too. More brilliant, edgy, or sizzling, ideally – but the difference should not be too large. For instance, some instruments may sound muddy, dull, or unclear when you play very softly or very low, or both. Or they may sound very shrill, thin, or metallic when you play loud, high notes. When playing the entire range of the instrument, loud or soft, the changes should be very gradual, and even the loudest notes should not break up or distort.

Not the same

When two people listen to the same horn, they often use very different words to describe what they hear. What one considers shrill and thin (and so not attractive), another may consider bright or brilliant (and so not unattractive). And what one describes as dark and velvety, another may think dull or stuffy. It all depends on what you like, and on the words you use to describe it. What sounds good to you and what doesn't, largely depends on what you like to hear and on the type of music you play.

Trombone: problem notes

If you are trying out a trombone with an F-attachment, do all your play-testing both with and without it. The almost unavoidable difference should be as small as possible. Two potential problem notes on trombones are high A-flat and the highest D: They have a tendency to come out less than even.

Small differences

Even two 'identical' trumpets may sound slightly different, regardless of their price range – so always buy the instrument you played, and not the 'same horn' from the warehouse.

SECONDHAND

There are lots of used instruments for sale, mainly because many players go on to buy a better horn after a few years. When you want to purchase a secondhand instrument, there are a few extra things to pay special attention to.

Your own mouthpiece

Take your own mouthpiece with you, if you have one. It's unlikely that you'll play comfortably with the mouthpiece that comes with the instrument. If you do buy a used mouthpiece, pay attention to the following: Most mouthpieces are silver-plated. If this protective coating is damaged or worn out, the brass below will make the mouthpiece taste bad. There's a chance of getting a rash too, as even the tiniest scratches can be home to even tinier bacteria. Some players aren't too bothered with a pitted or scratched mouthpiece rim: They like the extra bit of 'grip.'

With or without scratches, always clean a used mouthpiece before trying it out (see pages 64 and 95). Mouthpieces that aren't too badly damaged can be replated, which will usually cost some twenty to thirty dollars.

The lacquer

Used instruments may have patches where the lacquer has disappeared, as a result of sweat, rubbing, or both. These patches are very likely to make your hands smell of brass. Where there are scratches, even tiny ones, the lacquer can peel off, causing corrosion. Instruments can be relacquered or replated (see page 98).

The leadpipe

Remove the mouthpiece and the tuning slide to take a look through the leadpipe, which should be clean and perfectly smooth inside. On a flugelhorn, do the same with the tuning mouthpipe. On a trombone you can look through the first slide tube if you take the outer slide off. A really dirty leadpipe can only be cleaned in a special bath (see page 98).

Spots

Small round patches on the leadpipe may indicate that it's corroding from the inside out. Replacing a trumpet's leadpipe can easily cost a hundred dollars or more.

Dents

Dents – even small ones – can affect the instrument's intonation. The closer a dent is to the mouthpiece, the sooner it will be a problem.

Appraisals

Lumps of solder can be a sign of sloppy repairs. You may also come across instruments that have had parts replaced, such as a leadpipe or a bell. If you don't want to take any risks, have the instrument appraised (see page 29) before buying it.

Valves

While one player presses the valves straight down, another may push them a little to one side, making them wear slightly more in that direction. If your way of playing is very different from the previous owner's, the valves may feel different to you than they ever did to him or her – stiffer, for example.

Play

If you remove the valve caps and pull out the pistons a little, you shouldn't be able to move them sideways. If you can, they will probably leak. Getting valves repaired or replaced isn't cheap.

Plop

Suspect leaking valves? Pull out the valve slides one by one, without pressing down the valves. Every valve should produce a 'plop' when it comes off. If it doesn't, there's a problem. The leak may be in the valve or in the slide. The second valve slide especially can suffer from acidic perspiration, which can even cause tiny holes in the metal. If you have trouble getting the valve slides loose, try using a cloth (see page 98).

Water key

If you don't get a 'plop' from the third valve slide, the problem may be the water key, which is easy to repair or replace. To check the water key you take the third slide off; close one end with your finger and blow down the other end.

With one finger

Another leak test for the valves: Pull out the first tuning slide, depress the first valve, and blow through the instrument. If you put a finger on the tube the air is now coming from, there should be no leakage. Test the other valves in the same way.

Rotary valves

You can use this test for rotary valves too. Also feel how smoothly the rotor works, and check for excessive play. A tip: Opening and reassembling rotary valves requires experience and the right tools.

Rattles

Listen for rattles when playing the instrument. Also try the valves or rotors without playing. Unwanted noises can be the result of backlash, worn out felts, loose finger buttons, broken springs, and braces, for example.

Testing the hand slide   Tipcode TRP-008

Obviously, a trombone's slide should slide smoothly without leaking air. First check the water key: Take off the outer slide, close one end, and blow down the other. If that's okay, reassemble the slide, and rest its bend on your shoe. Close off both ends of the slide with your thumbs and quickly pull the inner slide upwards about ten or fifteen inches. If the outer slide doesn't come along right away, something is leaking. You can also hold the slide in the air, close off the inner slide, and then let go of the outer slide. If it falls straight-away, it leaks; take care it lands on a pillow, for instance. The first method is a little safer.

No slide lock

Slide locks are a fairly new addition to the instrument. If you are looking at an old instrument, check to see if it has

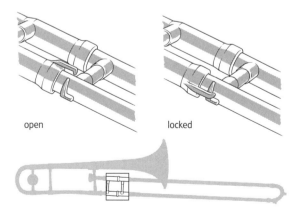

open   locked

A slide safety catch: not all older trombones have one.

one. If it does, try it out. Some slide locks are so smooth that they open by themselves.

Serial numbers and bore

To determine the age of a horn, you need to know its serial number. You'll usually find it on one of the valve casings or on the bell. Lists of serial numbers and the corresponding years of manufacture of many brands can be found on the Internet (see page 128), and in some brasswind stores. A few brands also put the bore size on the valve casings.

6. MOUTHPIECES

The mouthpiece you use should fit you properly, like a pair of shoes, and it should fit your horn too. A chapter about everything you may want to know to find the best one for your needs.

A mouthpiece that really suits you will allow you to get the tone you want with as little effort as possible. It'll make it easier to learn to play, to produce high and low notes, and to play in tune. It will also allow you to play for longer at a stretch.

Fit
A mouthpiece must suit your style of playing, as well as your embouchure and everything that goes with it – from the size and tension of your lips to your lung capacity, and the position of your teeth and jaws.

How it works
When you play, the rim of the mouthpiece rests against your lips. Your lips vibrate in the *cup*, and you blow the vibrating air into the instrument.

Main dimensions
Mouthpieces come in countless sizes and variations. The main 'parts' that determine how a mouthpiece will play and feel are:
- The bore or *throat*: the smallest opening of the mouthpiece.
- The width and shape of the edge or *rim* (*rim contour*).
- The diameter and depth of the cup.
- The *backbore*: the shape of the inside of the *shank*.

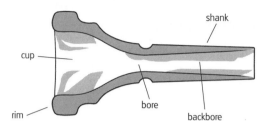

Medium

Many players start out on a 'medium' mouthpiece – one with a medium-sized rim, cup and bore. Most instruments are also sold with such mouthpieces. Of course, they are not necessarily the best solution for everybody. If you have rather soft, thick lips, a medium-sized rim is too narrow (it pinches), while for other lips it may be too wide (so that it gets in the way). The cup may be too small for you (so you don't get a good sound) or too big (so that you have to work too hard); or the bore is too small (which gives a poor response), or too big (making it hard to play in tune). And those are just a few examples...

Cheap

Cheaper instruments often come with a very small mouthpiece, because small ones are easier to play. One of the drawbacks? It's hard to develop a good embouchure with a mouthpiece that's too small.

Swapping or buying

When buying an instrument, most stores allow you to exchange the mouthpiece that comes with it. Good, pro-quality mouthpieces are available for thirty to fifty dollars; the top-of-the line models sell for over a hundred.

Fitting

A mouthpiece has all kinds of different dimensions, and as a player you have quite a few yourself too. Obviously, there's no simple rule to determine which mouthpiece suits you best. Reading this chapter will help, and so can your teacher or a good – and patient – salesperson.

Your own mouthpiece

If you go out shopping for a new mouthpiece, always bring the one you're currently playing. Based on its dimensions and your requirements (a bigger tone, easier high notes, a darker sound, or whatever) a good salesperson will be able to limit the number of mouthpieces to choose from to a handful, rather than you having to try out dozens.

Sound

A mouthpiece is not only important to how you play but also, of course, to your sound. Classical players often select a 'large' mouthpiece, which produces a warm, big tone that blends well with the sound of the other instruments. If you play Latin or jazz, for instance, you may be better off with a 'small' mouthpiece with a shallow cup and a smaller bore, which gives you a crisper, more brilliant sound. A tip: The largest mouthpieces require a good player – and the smallest ones do too.

Hundredths of an inch

When it comes to mouthpieces, hundredths of an inch count: Even the smallest difference makes for a big difference. So when you go to buy a new mouthpiece it's best not to choose one that is a lot bigger or smaller than the one you are used to. A very different mouthpiece may seem great when you buy it, but the chances are you won't stick with it.

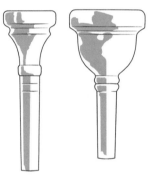

A trombone mouthpiece
(right) is a lot bigger.

Testing tips

The easiest way to select a mouthpiece is to keep comparing two or three at a time, just like with instruments. Try three, choose the one that feels best, replace the one you like least with another, and so on. Note that you won't get used to a new mouthpiece as easily as you would to a new instrument. Everything will feel different at first and you'll need some time to adapt your embouchure.

Fits the trumpet

Most trumpet mouthpieces physically fit most trumpets without a problem, but not all. A fairly long mouthpiece with a fairly thin shank may sometimes slide in so far that it touches the inner edge of the leadpipe. As a result, the mouthpiece won't fit snugly, and air may even leak out. If a mouthpiece won't go in far enough, your tone may suffer from the distance between the shank and the leadpipe edge.

Cornet mouthpieces
Cornet mouthpieces come in two lengths. American (long) cornets usually require the long type, of course.

Flugelhorn mouthpieces
Flugelhorn mouthpieces don't always fit either; for example, those with a fairly narrow shank are often too thin for American-made

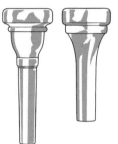

A long and a short cornet mouthpiece.

flugelhorns. Sometimes this can be solved with a special adapter, otherwise you'll have to find another mouthpiece.

Trombone mouthpieces
Trombone mouthpieces are available with a *large shank* for large-bore instruments and with a *small shank* for the smaller sizes.

Different teeth
Something quite different: Your front teeth are very important if you play a brass instrument. So before your dentist does anything drastic to them, tell him that you play. A tip: There are dentists who specialize in treating horn players.

Disinfectant
One more medical tip: If you are choosing mouthpieces together with a fellow horn player, you will minimize the risk of a rashes and other symptoms if you thoroughly clean the mouthpieces before swapping them. Special mouthpiece disinfectants are available. If one of you has a cold sore, don't exchange mouthpieces at all.

THE DIFFERENCES
What exactly are the differences between deep and shallow cups, large and small bores or narrow, wide, rounded, and

flat rims? What will gold-plating do for a mouthpiece and what difference does the weight of a mouthpiece make? These and many more questions are answered in the next sections.

Tricky

Mouthpieces come in hundreds of types and sizes. The fact that just about every manufacturer has its own system to identify the different models doesn't make life any easier. For instance, the Vincent Bach 7C, the Schilke 13B, and the Yamaha 11C4 are three trumpet mouthpieces with roughly the same dimensions, but very different names. Similarly, two 5A-mouthpieces by different brands may be nothing like each other.

The other way around

The only thing that all those names have in common is that the first figure tells you something about the cup diameter, and the letter that follows refers to the cup depth. Does that help you much? Not really: With one brand, a high number means a large diameter, and on another it means a small one. Likewise, the letter A can mean a deep cup or a shallow one, depending on which brand you are looking at…

More

Some mouthpieces have a longer code. An example would be a 12A4a: The second figure (4) refers to the shape of the rim (usually between 1 and 5, from very round to almost flat); the last letter refers to the backbore. This will often be between 'a' and 'e', from narrow to wide.

Comparable types

Fortunately, however, mouthpiece catalogs often list 'similar' models made by other companies. In addition, many brochures tell you the diameter and depth of the cup, and the shape and width of the rim.

Descriptions

Some catalogs also describe the sound characteristics of each or their models – but note that describing mouthpiece characteristics is as hard and subjective as describing flavors or sounds. Also, these descriptions tend to highlight the positive characteristics (high notes become much easier…), while leaving out the negative ones (… but low notes will be extremely hard to play).

The same?
If you play both trumpet and flugelhorn, for instance, you may have noticed that some brands use the same codes for their trumpet and flugelhorn mouthpieces. However, that doesn't guarantee that they're similar mouthpieces. In other words: If you're perfectly happy with a 5A of a particular brand on your trumpet, their flugelhorn-5A is not necessarily your best choice.

The whole thing
In mouthpieces, all dimensions are interrelated. For instance, you don't find mouthpieces with huge cups and very small bores, or the other way around. Even so, two mouthpieces with the same cup and the same bore may have slightly different characteristics – for instance, because one brand gives that type of mouthpiece a much bigger backbore than another.

And then there's this
Because everything is connected with everything else, and also with how you play, it's not always easy to find what you're looking for. One more example? For a more powerful, bigger sound you need a wider cup. But if the bore that goes with it is too big for you, you can run out of air at a stroke. Big sound? No. Big sigh.

Sound, feel, and play
So each change in one thing affects everything else in a mouthpiece. Still, to get a better idea of what mouthpieces are about, it's good to have a look at how various dimensions influence the sound they're likely to produce, and the way they feel or play.

THE CUP
For trumpets and cornets, the cup diameter can vary from about 0.59" to 0.69" (15–17.5 mm). For a tenor trombone, you add about 0.4". If letters are used to designate cup size, then 'C' usually indicates a medium cup.

Big

It takes a good player to handle a mouthpiece with a really big cup. Otherwise, it will be difficult to play in tune and to play large intervals (from high to low notes and the other way around), and you will quickly get out of breath.

Small

If the cup is too small for you, then your lips can't vibrate freely. Your timbre will suffer, and you'll be more likely to miss notes. A small cup may make hitting the highest notes a little easier, though – but if it's too small, you can forget them altogether.

The biggest you can handle

One thing that just about everyone agrees on is that you should choose the biggest cup diameter you can handle with your embouchure. This helps to increase your control, endurance, and tone quality.

Tip

The cup flares out a little at the top. The higher up you measure it, the bigger the cup diameter will appear. That's why two cups labeled 0.60" may actually have different sizes.

Thick lips

Some experts say that big lips require a big cup diameter, and vice versa. That seems pretty obvious – but lots of successful musicians have proven that it doesn't need to work that way.

A deep, wide cup, and a smaller, shallower one.

Cup depth

Cups also differ in their depth. A deeper cup is harder work to play, but you may get a warmer, bigger, darker tone in return. A shallow cup, like a smaller one, is less tiresome to play, and gives a brighter, edgier tone. High notes are easier to hit, but you may loose some tone in the lower registers, as well as some volume. Mouthpieces with adjustable cups are available too.

Cup shape

The cup of trumpet, cornet, and trombone mouthpieces is basically U-shaped on the inside, while the cup of a flugelhorn mouthpiece is shaped much more like a V. The more a cup of any type of mouthpiece tends toward a V-shape, the warmer, mellower, and less bright or edgy the tone will be, and vice versa.

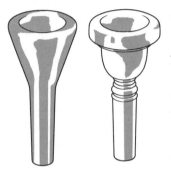

Two very similar cups on two very different mouthpieces.

Cup 1, cup 2

Some brands refer to the *first cup* (the upper part of the cup) and the *second cup* (the lower part). For example, a mouthpiece with a relatively narrow first cup makes high notes easier, while the tone will stay nice and dark due to a rather wide second cup.

THE RIM

The rim, which you hold against your lips, is especially important for how a mouthpiece feels. The width is usually somewhere between 0.200" and 0.240" (5–6 mm). Again add about 0.04" for tenor trombones.

Wide or narrow

The wider the rim is, the more the pressure is spread across your lips. That means a thicker rim is less tiring to play. This explains why really wide, flat rims are referred to as *cushion rims*. On the downside, a wide rim offers less control over the sound and the pitch, and high notes become harder to play. If you need to take the instrument from your mouth to play large intervals (from really high to really low notes, or vice versa), you may want to try a mouthpiece with a narrower rim.

Round or flat

With thick, soft lips you are more likely to need a wide rim with a rather flat contour. A narrow rim with a high-point, rounded contour can make both small and large intervals easier, and high notes will be easier to hit, possibly expanding your range. On the downside, it can pinch your lips and reduce your endurance.

Rim bite

Even the shape of the inner edge (*rim bite*) makes a difference. A sharper rim bite increases the response and facilitates the attack, but sliding from note to note may become harder, as

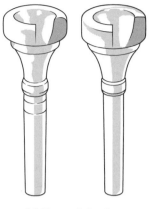

A fairly rounded and a fairly flat rim.

does playing for a long time. A smooth rim bite is more comfortable, but attacking notes becomes harder, as does playing in tune, and air and saliva may escape while you play...

An easy mistake

Some mouthpieces feel bigger or smaller than they really are, because of the position of the highest point of the rim. If this point is toward the outside of the rim, it will make the mouthpiece feel bigger than it actually is, and vice versa.

The same rim

Most horn players who play more than one instrument (*i.e.*, players who *double*) choose a mouthpiece with the same shape of rim for each horn. That makes switching instruments easier. If you can't find a mouthpiece with the rim you're looking for, there are specialists who can make or copy one for you.

Mouthpiece with interchangeable parts (Stomvi).

Combination mouthpiece

So-called *combination mouthpieces* come with several different shanks, a set of cups, and one rim, so you can use the same rim all the time, choosing a different cup or a different shank for each instrument you play. And if you need a brighter sound for a certain room, band or sound, you just use a smaller cup than the one you usually play.

THE BORE

The bore or throat is the smallest opening of the mouthpiece. It must be big enough to let the air pass through, while being small enough to provide sufficient resistance.

Large or small

Other than that, the influence of the bore is similar to what bore sizes elsewhere on the instrument do. If you want a flexible, free-blowing instrument, lots of volume, and easy low notes, go for a large bore – but you'll need more air and a well-developed embouchure. A smaller bore makes for a brighter sound; it increases the playing resistance and enhances the response of the instrument; also, the high register becomes easier to play. If it gets too small, however, the mouthpiece may seem to 'shut off' when you try to play the highest notes.

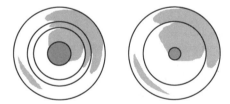

A mouthpiece with a large bore and a wide rim, and one with a small bore and a narrow rim; the opposite combination is equally possible.

Bore sizes

Just to give you an idea: The bore of trumpet and cornet mouthpieces range from about 0.140" to 0.160" (3.5–4 mm). On flugelhorns, the latter is an 'average' size. The bore of trombone mouthpieces range from about 0.215" to 0.300". Some brands use numbers to indicate bore sizes; on a trumpet mouthpiece, for example, a 22 indicates a narrow bore, and a 27 would be pretty wide.

THE BACKBORE

Backbores can have various designs, from V-shaped to barrel-shaped. By far the majority are V-shaped. If you have a lot of air, you may benefit from a barrel-shaped backbore. The opposite design (though it's very rare) may be a solution if you have very little air.

Bigger, smaller

Apart from that, the backbore behaves in a similar way to the bore. The 'narrower' it is, the brighter the sound. The 'wider' it is, the darker and mellower the sound – an open backbore is often referred to as a symphonic backbore. Some brands offer their mouthpieces with a choice of different backbores.

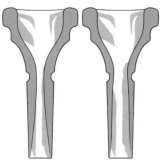

A narrow, V-shaped backbore and an open, slightly barrel-shaped backbore.

WEIGHT

All kinds of benefits are attributed to extra weight in a mouthpiece. That is why several brands sell mouthpieces in two versions: an 'ordinary' one and a weighted version. The latter cost a little more, and often come with descriptive names like Mega Tone (Bach) or Heavytop (Denis Wick).

Boosters

Rather than buy a weighted mouthpiece, you can get a *mouthpiece booster*.
Some boosters resemble big, separate cups, which you push onto the mouthpiece; others look like nothing more than a set of metal rings.

The same

The extra weight in a mouthpiece may help you produce

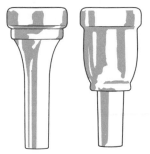

An ordinary cornet mouthpiece (short model) and a weighted version.

anything from an intensified, more stable tone with a solid core, to less distortion when playing really loudly; from a darker tone to more accuracy in the higher register. Also, it may increase your control over the entire range of the instrument. And as ever, there are the counter-arguments: A non-weighted mouthpiece enhances the response of your instrument and makes it easier to control and color the tone.

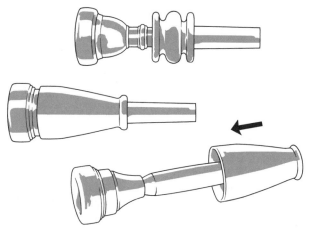

Various mouthpiece boosters (Wick, Holton).

MATERIALS
Most mouthpieces are made of silver-plated brass, but there are other materials to choose from.

Silver or gold
Brass leaves an unpleasant taste and can cause a rash, so the silver-plating is no mere luxury. If your skin or your lips can't cope with silver, or if you make silver tarnish quickly, a gold-plated mouthpiece may be the solution. They're expensive, though, and gold plating won't last as long as silver plating.

Plastic and wood
Another solution would be to buy a synthetic mouthpiece, or a metal one with a plastic rim, and there are pro-quality mouthpieces with a hard resin cup as well. Wooden mouthpieces, which are even rarer, give a very soft, mellow tone.

Solid silver and aluminum

Rather than a weighted silver-plated mouthpiece, you could go for a solid silver model. The sheer weight of this metal provides a stronger, darker sound. At the opposite end of the scale are ultra-light aluminum mouthpieces which respond very easily and offer bright highs.

AND FINALLY

You'll need to get used to a new mouthpiece, just as you would to a new pair of shoes. If you go straight ahead and play for hours with a new mouthpiece, you definitely risk sore lips. Another warning: Just as with the poorly-fitting shoes, it can take quite a while before you realize that your mouthpiece is causing problems. A tip: If you practice a lot but you aren't making any progress, it may not be down to your mouthpiece – but it very well could be.

Fifty or one

There are professional horn players who still use the mouthpiece their teacher gave them thirty years ago. There are others who have tried at least fifty different models and are still looking for the perfect one. There's a fair chance these players will never find it. There's also a good chance that the first category of horn player has an 'easy embouchure' and the second type doesn't. Or that the second type is more into experimenting... Tips on buying used mouthpieces are on page 57.

Brands

Vincent Bach, Burbank, Marcinkiewicz (MMP), Schilke, and Yamaha are some well-known mouthpiece manufacturers that also make instruments. Other instrument brands also have their own mouthpieces, which they don't necessarily design or make themselves. Then there are brands that supply only mouthpieces, and sometimes other brasswind products as well. Greg Black, Bush, Curry, Giardinelli, Faxx, Josef Klier, Laskey, Jet-Tone, Bob Reeves, Stork, Warburton, and Denis Wick are some well-known examples. Some brands that supply special mouthpieces are Jerwyn (adjustable cups), Jaztec (hard resin cup), Asymmetric (asymmetric cup to enhance the high range), and Parduba (double cup).

7. MUTES

The only mutes that really mute, so much so that the sound is muffled almost completely, are the practice mutes discussed in Chapter 3. All other types of mute are mainly used to create special effects, and timbres that range from razor-sharp to velvety-soft.

Most types of mutes are hollow cones in various sizes and shapes. They're held in place in the bell by a few strips or a ring of cork. The three best-known types are the *straight mute*, the *cup mute*, and the *harmon mute*. The exact effect of each of these types differs per brand, of course.

Straight mute

Tipcode TRP-009

The most commonly used type is the straight mute. If a

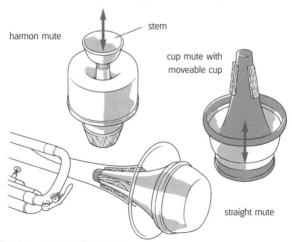

harmon mute — stem

cup mute with moveable cup

straight mute

The three most popular mutes.

classical piece specifies that you should play *con sordino* (with mute), you will be required to use this model. It largely closes off the bell, making your instrument sound a little like talking while holding your nose – slightly nasal and a bit thin or shrill.

Cup mute
Tipcode TRP-010

The cup mute looks like a straight mute with a cup. The inside of the cup is often finished with thin, soft material that slightly muffles the sound. Some models have an adjustable cup. The closer it is to the bell, the more it mutes the sound and the 'smaller' the sound becomes. Some cup mutes can double as practice mutes: See if you can move the cup right up against the bell.

Harmon, wah-wah, wow, bubble...
Tipcode TRP-011

The third popular type of mute comes with a host of different names, from harmon mute to *wow, wow-wow* or *wah-wah mute, bubble mute, extending tube,* or *E.T. mute.* It has a cork ring that closes off the bell entirely, the sound coming out of a hole in the mute only. As with the straight mute, the effect is often called 'nasal' – but it is very different. A little more metallic, you could say. Want to hear it? Listen to some of the older recordings of the late jazz trumpeter Miles Davis.

Laurel & Hardy

Harmon mutes virtually always come with a small adjustable pipe which you can stick into the hole. By opening and closing the hole of the stem with your hand you get the 'bubble' trumpet noises often used in Laurel & Hardy or other slapstick movies.

Aluminum, wood or plastic

Most mutes are made of aluminum, which produces a brighter, edgier sound than wood or fiberboard mutes. Some aluminum mutes have copper or brass bottoms, which make the sound more powerful or full. The sound of a plastic mute is usually somewhere between metal and wood. Plastic models are usually cheaper and more resilient than aluminum ones. You may occasionally see mutes made entirely of steel, copper, or another metal, which weigh and cost more.

Prices

Most mutes cost between fifteen and fifty dollars. The cheapest ones are usually made of fiberboard or plastic; the most expensive are special aluminum mutes, say with a copper bottom. Trombone mutes always cost a little more.

A plunger.

Plunger
Tipcode TRP-012

There are many other types of mutes. The *plunger*, for example, is so called simply because it looks like one. This type of mute is used for *doo-wah* effects. At the 'doo' you smother the sound by closing the bell, and at the 'wah' you take the mute off. Some bands use hats, known as *Derby mutes*, instead of rubber or metal plungers.

Bucket mute

As you would expect, a *bucket mute* is a small bucket that is usually attached to the edge of the bell with three small clamps. It's filled with a soft material such as mineral (rock) wool or foam plastic, which makes for a soft, smooth tone – that's why bucket mutes often have the word 'velvet' in their names. If you want a flugelhorn-like sound on a trumpet, you can do worse than try a bucket mute. This

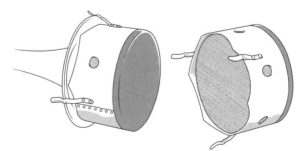

Bucket mute or velvet mute.

type of mute is available in various depths. The deeper it is, the more pronounced the effect.

Much more

And there's much more: For example, there are foldable and washable neoprene mutes that fit over your bell, or even over another mute. Lots of mutes come with very descriptive names, from the *clear-tone mute*, which looks like two straight mutes fitted together, to the sweet sounding *mel-o-wah*, the buzzing *wee-zee*, the penetrating *megaphone*, and the whispering *whispa-mute*...

MORE ON MUTES

A mute not only makes your instrument sound different, it makes it play differently too. You have to work harder, your volume goes down and the pitch often goes up a little. You'll notice this most with the lower notes. If they become sharp because of the mute, just pull your tuning slide out a little. The amount you need to fine-tune, and the increase in blowing resistance, depend on the design and the material of the mute. Badly-designed mutes can make it very hard to play in tune.

Your tongue

A mute must fit into or around the bell of your instrument properly. If it won't stay in place, don't use any force but instead moisten the cork strip(s). No tap handy? Then use your tongue.

Mute holder

There are various types of mute holders, which can hold one, two, or more mutes – or a drink. Most mute holders are designed to clamp to the tube or the music ledge of a music stand.

Brands

A few large, well-known makes of mutes are Tom Crown, Humes & Berg, Jo-Ral, and Denis Wick, and a few smaller ones are Charles Davis, Harmon, Spivak, and the Swedish Ullvén brand.

8. BEFORE AND AFTER

Before you start playing, you need to make sure that your valves or your slide are properly lubricated, and you'll tune your instrument. Taking a little care of your instrument when you stop playing may save you a lot of maintenance later. This chapter focuses on everything you do before and after playing, and includes tips on cases, gig bags, instrument stands, amplifying your instrument, and tips for on the road.

If you really want to keep your instrument in good condition, you'll need to do some work on it at home too. This is covered in Chapter 9.

Out of the case, mouthpiece on
Preferably lift a trumpet, cornet, or flugelhorn out of its case by the valve casings. Insert the mouthpiece into the leadpipe with a light twisting motion. Don't push or knock it in, as it may get stuck that way.

Assembling a trombone   Tipcode TRP-013
Always grasp the bell section of a trombone by the bell stay. Grasp the slide by the inner and outer braces to prevent the outer slide from slipping off. Now hold the slide with the bow downwards and fit the bell into it with the other hand.

Perpendicular
Make sure the bell section is exactly perpendicular to the slide, and only then – lightly – tighten the bell lock nut. If you twist the bell into its perpendicular position after

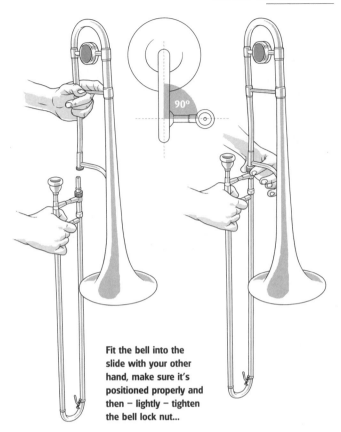

Fit the bell into the slide with your other hand, make sure it's positioned properly and then – lightly – tighten the bell lock nut...

you've tightened the nut, you may not be able to get it loose again: By twisting the bell, even slightly, you soon apply more force than you think. Only fit the mouthpiece once you have assembled your trombone.

Food and drinks

A tip in advance: If you want to make it as easy as possible to keep your horn clean, wash your hands and brush and floss your teeth before you play, and don't drink anything that contains sugar when you're playing.

VALVES AND SLIDES

Valves must always be lubricated using special valve oil. In order to do the job properly, you need to take the pistons out (see Chapter 9, which also covers the various lubricants).

Upside down

If a piston valve gets a little slow, you are overdue in oiling it. A quick solution is to hold your instrument upside down and to drip a little valve oil into the holes of the bottom caps while moving the pistons. If you use too much oil, most of it will probably run straight out again.

Rotary valves

Oiling a rotary valve always takes more time, so you're better off doing it before the gig, and preferably at home (see page 93).

Trombone slides

Lubricating your trombone slide, too, is a job best done at home. Turn to page 94 to read how. Just before playing, use a special spray bottle to sprinkle some cool, clear tap water over the inner slide. This makes it move as smoothly as it can. There are all kinds of special agents that can be added to the water – some trombonists are convinced they help, others prefer to do without. A tip: Always empty the spray bottle before you put it in your case.

TUNING

Tuning your instrument is really very easy: You simply move the tuning slide out until you get exactly the right pitch. The hard part of tuning, however, is to learn to hear when the pitch is right, and to play the required note without pitch fluctuations.

Too cold

If your instrument is very cold, it may sound flat, even with the tuning slide pushed fully in – so you'll have to

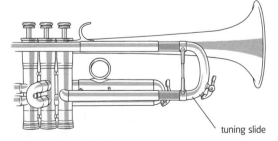

tuning slide

The extended tuning slide of a trumpet...

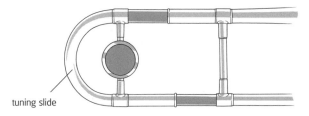

tuning slide

... and of a trombone.

warm it up. Do this by breathing soundlessly through it (as if you're using the water keys, but less vigorously...), or simply by playing the instrument for a while. A cold mouthpiece feels uncomfortable: Keep it in your pocket or hold it in your hand to warm it up. If you have to play outside and it's cold, you may use a lip saver: a soft, thin cover that slides over your mouthpiece.

Tuned to A

Many orchestras and bands tune to the A4, which is the A above Middle C (see page 15). If you play that note on a piano, the strings vibrate 440 times per second.

A=440   Tipcode TRP-014

This pitch is indicated as A=440 hertz, 440Hz, or 440 vps (vibrations per second). You can hear it with the Tipcode above.

Tuning fork   Tipcode TRP-015

If you don't have a piano at hand, the most affordable way to get this reference pitch is to buy a tuning fork. Tap its prongs against your knee, set the stem against your ear or on a table, and you'll hear a concert A. (Tuning forks in other tunings are available as well.) Electronic metronomes can often play this pitch too.

A tuning fork.

Concert A or B-flat

On a trumpet, a flugelhorn, or a cornet, you get a concert A by playing a B. Bands with lots of B-flat instruments may tune to concert B-flat – so you play a C.

Trombone

On a trombone you play the A with the slide in the second position. An F-attachment needs to be tuned separately. It has its own tuning slide.

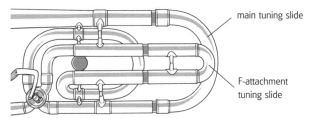

main tuning slide

F-attachment tuning slide

The F-attachment needs tuning too...

How far?

Learning to tune your instrument takes time. First, you'll have to learn to hit the desired note (A or B-flat) without pitch fluctuations. Second, you may have trouble hearing whether you're sharp (so you have to extend the tuning slide) or flat (so you have to push it in, raising the pitch).

Practice   Tipcode TRP-016

A tip to practice hearing pitch differences: Play a note with the tuning slide fully extended (take care it doesn't slip off). Then push it in all the way and play the same note again. It will sound noticeably higher, maybe only after some practice. If you hear the difference, reduce the distance you move the tuning slide, so the resulting pitch difference will be smaller – and try to hear what happens.

An inch

Another tip: To tune to A=440 on a trumpet, you probably don't have to extend the tuning slide more than an inch. Fine-tuning is often a matter of tenths of an inch or less.

Tuners

You can also use an electronic tuner – a small device that shows you whether you're sharp, flat, or in tune. Most tuners have a small microphone built in, but you can also get tuners that 'feel' the pitch when you clamp them to your instrument. This type of tuner responds only to what you play, rather than responding to the notes of the rest of the band too.

New mouthpiece?

A new mouthpiece may require a different 'standard' position of your tuning slide, either because it slides further or less far into the receiver, or because it has a different bore, cup, or backbore size.

Weak

If you need to extend the tuning slide almost fully, for instance because you have to tune to a very low-pitched piano, you won't just get a lower note. Your sound will become weak and uncentered, and the intonation of your instrument will suffer: Notes may start to deviate more than usual.

A little higher   Tipcode TRP-017

Some orchestras tune just a little higher, for instance to A=442. There are tuning forks that produce that pitch too, and electronic tuners can often be adjusted to different pitches.

... AND AFTER

It's easiest to keep a mouthpiece clean by simply rinsing it with lukewarm water after playing. If your case or gig bag doesn't have a mouthpiece holder, keep it in a leather or synthetic pouch; these sell for some five to fifteen dollars, usually with a zipper or a snap closure. Molded pouches are also available, as well as models that hold two or more mouthpieces.

Not on its rim

Always set your mouthpiece down on its side, never on its rim. This prevents scratches and dents – as long as it doesn't roll off the table.

Removing moisture

When you play, you'll use your water key(s) to remove most of the condensation that collects in your instrument. After the performance, it's best to get rid of the rest of it too. Remove the valve slides, and then blow through the instrument, as if you were using the water key(s). A tip: When pulling out a valve slide, prevent wear by depressing the corresponding valve.

The dryer it is

The better you dry the parts of your instrument after playing, the less maintenance your horn will require and the longer it will last. Some horn players leave their cases open when they get home, so that everything can dry some more. A tip: After playing, push your tuning slide in all the way. If you don't, it may get stuck in the long run.

Cloth

Sweat can damage lacquer, brass, and silver. So run a soft, lint-free cloth over your instrument after playing, and don't forget the inside of the bell. An old T-shirt (unprinted) or an old dish cloth will do fine.

CASES AND BAGS

New instruments usually come with a basic rectangular case that features one or more holes to put your mouthpiece(s) in, and a separate pocket for valve oil and other accessories. A plush or velvet lining prevents scratches. If your instrument didn't include a case, or if you want another one, here's what you can choose from.

More space

Good hard-shell cases usually have a strong plywood or molded plastic core. The rectangular models have more space than others. Larger cases even allow you to store one or more mutes, a music stand, and sheet music, and there are special cases that are big enough to hold two instruments. Double-wall cases offer extra protection. Trombone cases flare out at the bell. They should always match the instrument's bell size; this can vary quite a lot (see page 37).

Prices

Basic trumpet cases start at around fifty or seventy-five dollars, but you can easily go up to six times as much, or more. Shaped or contoured cases, usually with a hard plastic shell, may be just as strong, but they offer less space.

Gig bag

A *gig bag* is a thickly lined bag, often made of water-resistant synthetic cloth, and slightly shaped for the instrument. Gig bags often have one or more extra pockets, as well as shoulder or backpack straps. You can buy a decent one for around fifty dollars, but prices can go up to a hundred fifty or more for special designs (*e.g.*, holding two or three instruments) or materials (*e.g.*, leather). Most gig bags won't protect your instrument as well as a good case does, but gig bags are more comfortable to carry around.

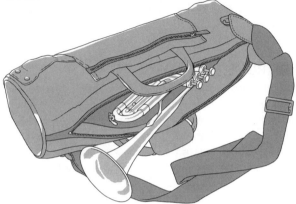

A gig bag with a shoulder strap.

Conceal the shape
If you don't want everyone to know that you have one or more instruments with you, you can also get carryall bags that conceal their shape – unless you happen to play the trombone.

Locked
Most cases can be locked. More than anything, these small locks are there to prevent the lid from springing open if the case falls. A separate case cover (Cordura, canvas, leather) will do that too, as well as offering additional protection against rain and dirt.

Locks and hinges
Check to see how sturdy latches, locks, zips, hinges, and handles look: They tend to be the weak points on cases and gig bags. Plastic clips and rings may not be as strong as metal ones.

Too hot

Always store your instrument in its case or bag, rather than leaving it on a table or a chair. Never leave an instrument where it can get too hot: High temperatures can cause valves and valve slides to jam, and brass gets hotter than you might think in the sun.

Backpack

If you are transporting your case or bag in a backpack, always pack it so that the bell is pointing upwards.

INSTRUMENT STANDS

If you take a break, it's best to put your instrument in its case or bag, or else put it on a stand. Most trumpet stands are simple tripods with a wooden or plastic peg, over which you slide the bell of your instrument. For a flugelhorn you need one with a larger peg. The very smallest trumpet stand is designed so that it fits the bell of your horn when folded up. A tip: Five-legged stands are less easily kicked over than the standard three-legged designs.

Trombone stands

Trombone stands are larger, of course. When folded up, they're usually the size of a music stand. Stands mainly differ in how easily and small they fold up, in how sturdy they are, and in how much stability they offer.

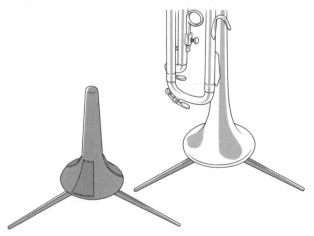

Mini stand for trumpet and cornet; folds up and fits inside the bell.

No stand

If you don't use a stand, always put down a trumpet or cornet on its left side to prevent damaging the vulnerable second valve slide.

AMPLIFIED BRASS

Most good vocal microphones work well for brass instruments. Using a microphone on a regular stand has one disadvantage: You can hardly move without influencing the volume or the tone perceived by your audience.

Clip-on microphone

One solution is to use a small clip-on microphone that attaches to the instrument, allowing you to move as much as you want. Prices usually range from two to five hundred dollars; wireless systems are usually more expensive.

Preamplifier

The signal produced by these clip-on microphones needs to be boosted before it can be sent to the main amp. The required preamplifier, which often features at least a volume control, is a small box that you usually attach to your clothing or belt.

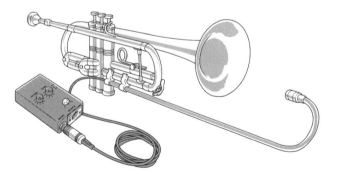

Trumpet microphone with clamp and preamplifier (SD Systems).

Effects

Brass players use far fewer electronic effects than electric guitarists do, but the use of a *reverb* and a *delay* is quite common. Other effects (e.g., *flangers*, *wah-wahs*, or a *chorus*) can be fun to experiment with.

ON THE ROAD

When you travel with your instrument, which includes visits to your teacher, you may find the following tips helpful:

- In the car, your instrument is safest **between the back and front seats**. The worst place is under the rear window, especially on a sunny day.
- When using public transportation, keep your horn **on your lap**. It's safe, and you won't forget it this way.
- Flying out? Then take it along as **hand luggage**.
- If you still leave your horn behind somewhere, you're more likely to get it back if your **name, address, and phone number** are listed inside your case or bag.
- Consider **insuring your instrument**. Musical instruments fall under the insurance category of 'valuables.' A regular homeowner insurance policy will usually not cover all possible damage, whether it occurs at home, on the road, in the studio, or onstage.
- To get your instrument insured you'll need to know the **serial number** (see page 60) and some other details, which you can list on pages 130–131 of this book. Insurance companies may also require an appraisal (see page 29) and proof of purchase.

9. MAINTENANCE

Your instrument will sound and look better for longer and it will hold its value better if you clean it regularly. Also, valves and slides need to be lubricated from time to time. Other than that, brass instruments require little maintenance. Besides tips on jobs you can do yourself, this chapter suggests what you should leave to a professional.

Keeping the outside of your instrument clean is very simple. There are all kinds of treated cloths and even polishing gloves that not only clean your instrument, but make it shine too. Some even add a thin film that protects it against sweat and dirt. Of course, a regular cotton cloth with a little instrument cleaner will do the job as well.

Lacquer or silver

There are different cloths, gloves, and cleaners for lacquered and silver-plated instruments, and only a few that you can use for both. Using the wrong type may damage your lacquer or plating. Ordinary silver polish or brass polish is cheaper than most polishes sold in music shops, but it isn't the same stuff: It's too abrasive, leaving scratches and removing the lacquer finish.

Blacker is better

Silver polishing cloths get very black in time. Contrary to what you might think, the blacker they get, the more effective they'll be. Washing a silver polishing cloth turns it into an ordinary piece of cloth, so don't. Silver-plated instruments should be polished very rarely in order to

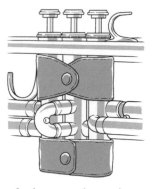

A valve cover, valve guard, or hand guard.

avoid wearing down the extremely thin plating.

Valve covers

If you have very acidic perspiration, you may find dull spots where you hold the instrument. The solution is a slip-on *valve cover*, available in vinyl and leather. The latter type costs a little more, but is more comfortable.

Trombonists

Similar covers are available for trombones. Many horn players have alternative ways to protect the vulnerable parts of their instruments, one of them being to wind them with duct tape. That won't look or feel as good as leather and you may have trouble getting it off again after a while – and it only saves you a couple of dollars.

VALVES AND SLIDES

Valve slides shouldn't move as easily as pistons; piston valves need a thinner type of oil than rotary valves; and so on... Perfectionists may use six or seven different lubricants for the various parts of their instrument, but others happily make do with two. That is probably the minimum, though. There is no one 'best way' to lubricate your instrument. Just ask other horn players for their experiences and try a few different brands and methods yourself.

In advance

Some tips in advance:

- Most lubricants cost around five dollars per bottle, so that shouldn't stop you from experimenting a bit.
- Most people use too much oil, rather than too little. Usually, one or a few drops will do. Excess oil and grease can be removed with a special degreaser.
- There are lubricants that do no contain oil. They're smooth and odorless, and can't stain your clothes – but

some say they're a bit slower than traditional lubricants: The valves don't come back as fast.

Valve oil

To keep your piston valves moving smoothly you need valve oil, a lubricant which is almost as runny as water. Some piston valve lubricants are as odorless as water too. How often you should oil your valves depends on many things: the quality of the instrument, the piston and valve materials, and even on how your saliva affects the type of oil you use – another reason to try various lubricants.

Right

You can lubricate your valves without taking the pistons out (see page 80), but it's better to remove them. Do so one by one, and be careful: They're hollow, and their thin walls are easily dented. First wipe the piston clean with a lint-free cloth, then apply three or four drops of oil to it and replace it with a light twisting motion. That way the oil will spread around the whole piston and the inside of the valve casing, and you can easily feel the piston guide or guides (see page 46–47) slot into place.

Wrong

If you don't reassemble the valve properly, or if you put pistons in the wrong casings, the instrument will either sound like a lousy Donald Duck imitation, or like nothing

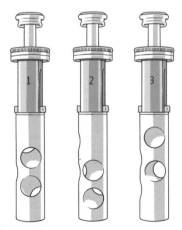

... see if they have numbers.

at all. A tip: Only tighten the valve cap after you've made sure that the piston has been properly reassembled. If you do remove all three pistons at once, remember which valve goes where. They are often numbered: If so, piston #1 is the one closest to the mouthpiece. Another tip: Valve caps will stay in place if you tighten them gently by hand. Don't use any force, let alone a wrench.

A little thicker

Some horn players find valve oil too runny, so they put a tiny bit of Vaseline on their valves. You're better off trying a slightly thicker type of oil, though, because Vaseline can eventually make your pistons stick.

Top cap felts

In the long run, the felt washers on top of the valves (*top cap felts*) will wear out. If they have become too thin, the pistons will go down too far – and you may even not notice that the horn's resistance gets bigger, because it happens so gradually. Want to check your felts? Remove the second valve slide, depress the second valve, and look: The ports should be perfectly in line with the tubing. If the piston goes down too far, the felts need to be replaced.

Leadpipe

To protect your leadpipe and receiver from corrosion due to the acids in your saliva, occasionally trickle a few drops of valve oil into them. A tiny drop on the thread of each valve cap will prevent them from getting stuck.

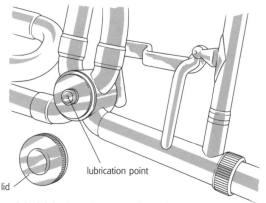

lubrication point

lid

One of the lubrication points on an F-attachment.

Rotary valves

Rotary valves need a slightly heavier lubricant. Rotors can be lubricated from the outside. Most of them require you to first unscrew a cap on one side and a screw on the other, but you don't need to dismantle it entirely.

Through the tube
Tipcode TRP-018

You can also lubricate rotary valves by removing the appropriate slide and trickling a few drops of oil into the tubing which leads to the rotor. The oil will distribute best if you then operate the valve for a little while. A tip: Some brands offer a separate lubricant for the valve lever.

String-action F-attachment

If you have a string-action F-attachment, check occasionally to make sure the string is not about to break, and be sure to always have a spare string with you, as well as the required tool or tools (usually a screwdriver will do) and a sketch of how to fit the string. Without a proper illustration, fitting a string is nearly impossible – even for some experienced players. Check if there's one in your instrument's manual. The illustration shown here may deviate from the one you need for your instrument.

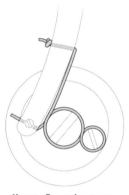

How to fit a string to an F-attachment.

Valve slides

Valve slides, on trumpets, cornets, and flugelhorns, should not slide as easily as the pistons. Therefore, slide oil or slide grease is less runny than valve oil. Because you use them while you play, the adjustable (third and first) valve slides need to move a little more easily than the tuning slide or the second valve slide. Some brands have lighter and heavier types of slide oil for that purpose; others offer special tuning-slide oil.

Alternatively

You can also use the same slide oil for all the slides, and make the first and third valve slides a bit faster by using some valve oil as well. A tuning slide that moves of its own accord needs a heavier lubricant. Can the crook of a slide be removed? Then lubricate it occasionally, before it gets stuck.

Vaseline

Very frugal horn players use non-acidic Vaseline for the valve slides. It's cheaper than the 'official' lubes, but then a small pot of slide oil will last you ages, it's less sensitive to changes in temperature, and it does exactly what it's made for.

Lubricate, twist, replace

Remove the valve slide you want to lubricate from your instrument, carefully clean it with a soft, dry cloth and lubricate both inner tubes. Wipe away the excess oil so that it doesn't end up inside the instrument. Slide one of the inner tubes into its outer tube and twist it a couple of times to distribute the lubricant over the entire surface. Now take it out again, and do the same with the other end. Then put the slide back on. Usually there's only one way it'll fit. If you do it the wrong way around, the slide won't go in all the way, or not at all.

Trombone slide cream

The trombone slide requires its own lubricant. Use *trombone slide cream* daily on new slides; once the instrument is broken in you won't need to do it as often.

Skin cream

Trombonists, like other brass players, often experiment with alternative solutions. Some swear by certain types of furniture polish or skin cream instead of dedicated slide cream. Again: When you consider how long it lasts, a jar of dedicated slide cream isn't that expensive – and you can be confident it will always work well.

Never

The slide itself is only around a hundredth of an inch (0.25 mm) thick, so it dents and bends easily. To lubricate it, dismantle it carefully and lay the outer slide in your case. Wipe the tubes clean one by one, always toward the ends. A tip: Never hold one tube while you are cleaning or lubricating the other, to prevent bending them.

Rotate the tube

Next, spread a little cream around the first tube and wipe off the excess. Stick the tube into the outer slide and rotate it a few times. Take it off, and do the same with the second tube. If you're going to play right away, spray on a little water and go (see page 80).

The fast way

Some trombonists prefer to lubricate only the first half of both tubes, and then move the slide in and out a few times. That way there's less chance of dented and bent tubes, and the cream will spread around the slide anyway as you play.

Other parts

Now and again dab a little cream on the bell lock, the mouthpiece shank, and the slide lock. That way you'll avoid anything getting terribly stuck.

INSIDE

If you really want to do a proper job, you need to clean the inside of your instrument every two or three months. Your mouthpiece, receiver, and leadpipe require a little extra attention more often, as they are the first parts to get clogged up by whatever you blow into the instrument.

Mouthpiece

If you don't clean your mouthpiece now and then, the bore will gradually get smaller and smaller... Rinsing it under the tap (lukewarm or cold water only) after every session is a good start. About once a week, clean the mouthpiece with a special mouthpiece brush and a mild soap solution; liquid detergent will do just fine. Keep pulling the brush through the mouthpiece until it comes out clean.

Bowl

To remove scale, put your mouthpiece in a bowl of water with a good dash of vinegar once every few weeks. Another cleaning trick: Leave your mouthpiece to soak for a few hours in some water with liquid or dry detergent. Some horn players will even dissolve some baking soda in a pan and boil their mouthpiece in it. Do rinse your mouthpiece with lots of cold water before touching it: Brass gets very hot and doesn't cool off quickly.

Big tub

To clean the inside of your instrument, it's handy if you have a tub big enough to submerge it completely. Lay a towel on the bottom of the tub to prevent scratches, put your horn in (pistons should be removed), and fill the tub with lukewarm water. A trombone should always be bathed in three sections, preferably one at a time: the bell, the inner slide, and the outer slide. Rotary valves can stay in place.

Detergents

You may add a little mild shampoo to the water. Do not use anything that may be more aggressive. Some even consider a liquid detergent too much – but others have been using it for years. If you add anything, make sure to rinse the instrument afterwards.

Running water

If you don't have a big enough tub, allow some lukewarm water to run through each tube for little while. You can also do this to clean the receiver and leadpipe only. For that purpose, just take the tuning slide off (the hand slide, for trombone players).

Too hot

If the water is too hot, you may burn yourself as you touch the instrument. Also, hot water may damage a lacquer finish.

Cleaners, snakes, and brushes

The wet tubing can be cleaned inside using a bore cleaner or *snake*: a flexible coiled spring or nylon string with a hard

A bore cleaner, a valve brush, and a mouthpiece brush.

brush or a sponge at one or both ends. Similar products are available to clean the valve casings and the pistons' portholes. Alternatively, you can pull a clean cotton cloth through them a couple of times.

Spit balls
Another way to clean the inside of your instrument is to use Spit Balls – small foam balls which you blow through the tubing.

Drying and lubricating
Rinse out all the tubes again when they are clean. Shake (carefully…) and blow out as much water as you can, dry the outside, and leave everything until the inside is dry too. Then lubricate the valves and the slide(s), and don't forget to apply a tiny drop of oil to the shank of your mouthpiece, the inside of the leadpipe, and the moving parts of the water keys.

Scale and tarnish
To properly remove scale and tarnish from the inside of the instrument, you'll need to get it thoroughly cleaned by a professional (see page 98).

Maintenance sets
Many brands sell complete maintenance sets that contain various brushes, a cleaning cloth, lubricants, and sometimes even spare parts such as felts for the valves, or water key corks.

PROBLEMS
If your instrument is dented, if a brace has come loose, or if your mouthpiece, a valve, a slide, or anything else is stuck, the best advice is to take it to a technician. Bending, soldering, or using wrenches or other tools on your instrument is always risky, not least because brass instrument have very thin walls.

Stuck mouthpiece
You can sometimes get a stuck mouthpiece loose by running plenty of cold water over it. Wrapping a cloth around it will give you more grip. If that doesn't work, get

it to a technician, who will use a special mouthpiece puller. Should your instrument not fit its case or bag with the mouthpiece attached, wrap it in a towel for the time being.

Cloth   Tipcode TRP-019
If a valve slide is jammed, you may try to pull it out with a cloth, which you push through the bow. Be careful not to damage anything when the slide lets go: Keep hold of it when you pull. If you think you need to pull too hard, have a technician do it for you.

Overhaul
A proper overhaul is a job for a professional too. This includes replacing felts, springs, and corks, smoothing out dents, polishing the instrument, and everything else it needs to perform properly for another one, two, or three years – depending on how often you play and what you do to keep your horn clean. A complete overhaul also includes a special bath to remove inside scale and tarnish, as well as relacquering or replating the instrument, which will make it as good as new. This will usually set you back some two hundred fifty to three hundred fifty dollars or more.

10. BACK IN TIME

The trombone hasn't changed much over the last four centuries and even the valved trumpet is a good hundred and fifty years old. To meet their very earliest ancestors, you need to go back thousands of years.

Lip-vibrated wind instruments made of shells, hollowed-out pieces of wood, and animal horns have been around for thousands of years – the double meaning of the word 'horn' is no coincidence.

A horn literally made of horn, with holes for playing different notes.

Bronze, gold, silver

Only much later did the first metal variations appear, made of bronze, gold, or silver, for instance. Early metal trumpets were usually no more than a long straight tube, slightly wider at one end (the 'bell'), with the other end (the 'mouthpiece') flattened slightly for the lips.

A few examples

Over the centuries, just about every culture has had its own trumpets. From the Greek *salpinx*, the bronze Celtic *carnyx*, and the Roman *lituus*, over two thousand years ago, to the medieval European *buisine* and the fifteen-foot long, copper Tibetan *dung* – and those are just a few examples.

Bends without kinks

Only six hundred years ago did craftsmen learn how to bend tubes without getting kinks in them. By then, the trumpet gradually began to assume its modern form. It was still without valves, though, so it could play only a limited number of different notes (see page 4). These types of horns are known as *natural instruments*.

Without valves: a natural trumpet.

Slide trumpet

Not much later, someone came up with the *slide trumpet*, which allowed more notes to be played. It was awkward to play, as you had to slide the entire instrument backwards and forwards. The trombone (Italian for large trumpet), which came a little later, was a much better solution. Some of the earliest trombones, which are more than four centuries old, look remarkably like the modern-day instrument.

The first valves

In the eighteenth century, an anonymous instrument maker devised a system of keys for the trumpet, but it

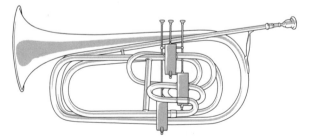

The earliest valves looked a bit like matchboxes.

wasn't ideal. The breakthrough for brass wind instruments came in 1815, when the German craftsmen Blühmel and Stölzel presented the first valve, which looked something like a metal matchbox. In 1839, the Frenchman Périnet added a few improvements, and since then piston valves have been known as *Périnet valves*. A few years earlier, the Austrian trumpet-maker Riedl had invented the rotary valve.

The flugelhorn...

Originally, the flugelhorn was a small horn played by the horsemen who rode on the far left and right flanks (Flügel, in German) of a hunting party. Long ago, some flugelhorns had keys, like a saxophone, and around 1850 the first flugelhorns with valves appeared. Who invented the modern flugelhorn will never be entirely clear: Numerous instrument makers came up with numerous designs and variations over the years, finally resulting in the present-day design. The original valveless flugelhorn, commonly referred to as bugle, is still being used (see page 107).

... and the cornet

Cornet means 'little horn'. The short cornet is a small French or German horn with valves added. In the US, players preferred a somewhat brighter, crisper sound, and so the long American cornet was designed.

11. THE FAMILY

Essentially, all brass instruments are very much alike. The main differences? The tubing may be longer or shorter, it may be more or less conical, and there may be one or more valves or a slide – and that's about it. A brief introduction to the most important family members.

To start with, many brass instruments come in various keys, such as the C trumpet mentioned in Chapter 2. But there are many others, especially among trumpets.

From soprano to bass

A little smaller than a C trumpet are the soprano trumpets in D, E-flat, or E. Another size smaller and higher is the sopranino. The very smallest and highest-sounding model is the piccolo trumpet or Bach trumpet, in A and B-flat. There are lower-sounding trumpets too – in F, for example, or the bass trumpet in B-flat, which has the same range as a tenor trombone.

Two tunings

Smaller trumpets often can be pitched in two keys, and some even in three. If you buy a G/F trumpet, for instance, it will probably come with two leadpipes, a set of extra valve slides, and an extra tuning slide, or even a second bell. When you are playing in F you use the longer tubes and valve slides, and if you need a G trumpet you use the shorter ones, which raise the pitch. Besides these trumpets, there are also flugelhorns that can be used in C and D, for instance. The more extra parts you get with it, the better the intonation of the instrument can be in both keys.

Four valves

Piccolo trumpets often have four valves; there are also flugelhorns with four. The fourth valve lowers the note by a fourth (from B-flat to F, for instance), just like an F-attachment on a trombone.

Pocket-sized

The *pocket trumpet* looks smaller than it is: If you were to roll it out, it would be just as long as a regular B-flat trumpet, and it sounds the same pitch too. Pocket-sized cornets are also available.

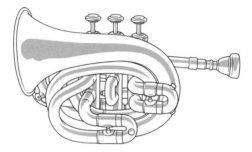

A pocket trumpet sounds bigger than it looks.

Rotary valves and rotary trumpets

Trumpets with rotary valves, commonly known as *rotary trumpets*, are still popular in some countries, mainly in Germany.

German trumpets

The rest of the instrument is usually different too. For example, rotary trumpets have a very large bore. Their big, powerful and warm sound makes them very suitable for symphonic works of German composers. Rotary trumpets

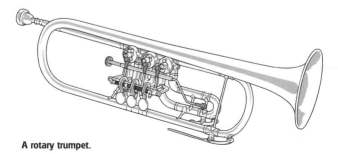

A rotary trumpet.

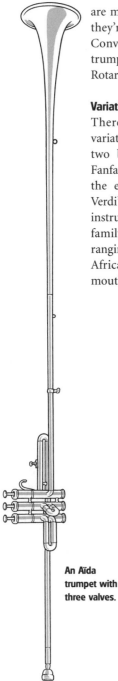

are most popular in that country – indeed, they're also known as *German trumpets*. Conversely, German musicians refer to trumpets with piston valves as *jazz trumpets*. Rotary flugelhorns are available too.

Variations

There are many, many more trumpet variations, such as 'stereo' instruments with two bells; or stretched instruments like Fanfare, Herald, or Triumphal trumpets, or the equally stretched Aïda trumpet from Verdi's 1871 opera. Many other lip-vibrated instruments, which all belong to the trumpet family, can be found in other cultures, ranging from side-blown horns (found in Africa, for instance) to the alphorn (no mouthpiece, no bends, no brass).

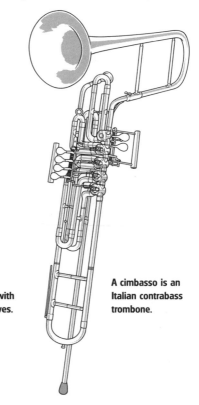

An Aïda trumpet with three valves.

A cimbasso is an Italian contrabass trombone.

Trombones

Besides the tenor, alto, and bass trombones, there are *soprano* or *mini trombones* in B-flat, plus the rare contrabass trombone or the *cimbasso*, the Italian contrabass.

A bit of everything

A few more variations: The Holton Superbone has two piston valves, like a trumpet, but it also has a slide, like a trombone. Or the Kanstul Flugelbone, which looks like a flugelhorn but sounds like a trombone. And then there's the flumpet, which is somewhere between a flugelhorn and a trumpet.

BACKGROUND BRASS

The instruments in this book belong to what's known as *soprano* or *treble brass* – the higher-pitched brass instruments – as opposed to the so-called *low brass* instruments. The bass trombone is a low brass instrument, and so are the tuba and the euphonium, among others. Most of these instruments are also known as *background brass*: instruments which are mainly used to accompany the melody instruments, and hardly ever for solos. They often have more valves, up to six, and they all have a markedly conical, widely-flared tube.

Tuba

The name *tuba* usually refers to the bass tuba, which has a tube around twenty-five feet long. Bass tubas come in C, for symphony orchestras, and in B-flat, for brass, concert and other wind bands. One size smaller are tubas pitched in F and E-flat. These low pitches are often indicated as CC, BB♭, FF, and EE♭, respectively, pronounced as double C, double B-flat, and so on.

Euphonium

The tenor tuba, pitched one octave higher than the bass tuba, is usually referred to as *euphonium*.

Saxhorns

Around 1845, when Adolphe Sax was still perfecting his saxophone, he was granted a patent on a whole family of *saxhorns*, from large to small. A few of those instruments

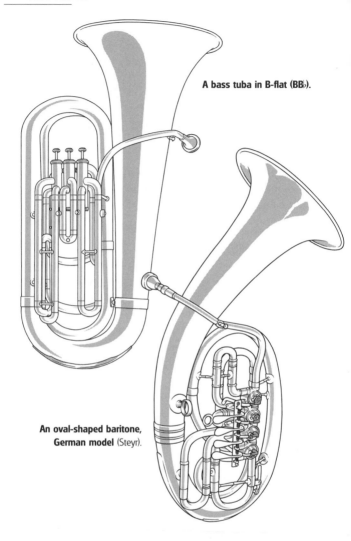

A bass tuba in B-flat (BB♭).

An oval-shaped baritone, German model (Steyr).

are still in use, such as the *tenor horn* and the *baritone*. The baritone is very similar to the euphonium, but a euphonium has a wider bore and a larger bell, and as a result sounds somewhat bigger and warmer. The two lowest-sounding saxhorns are pretty much the same instruments as the large B-flat and E-flat tubas.

Confusing

Many brass instruments have different names in different countries: A tenor horn is called alto or althorn by some, and baritone by others… Another difference: German saxhorns look quite different because of their oval shape – but they sound the same, basically.

French horn

Brass instruments are often called horns, but the only 'real' horns have a circular main tube. The *French horn*, a very distinctive instrument, is most often found in symphony orchestras, concert bands, and brass bands. The *mellophone* is very similar to this instrument. The *hunting horn* is a valveless horn (see page 107).

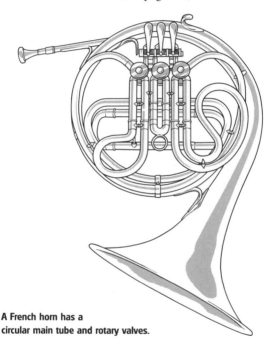

A French horn has a circular main tube and rotary valves.

OTHER RELATIVES

The brass family is much bigger still. For instance, there are special designs for marching bands, such as the famous sousaphone, and there is a whole group of natural instruments.

Marching instruments

Ordinary tubas, horns, and trombones are tricky to play if you're marching. That's why many special models have

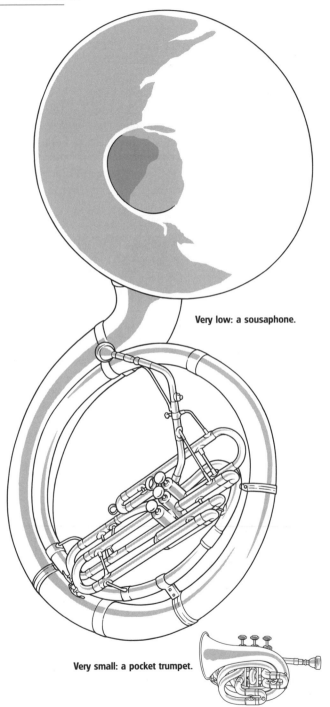

Very low: a sousaphone.

Very small: a pocket trumpet.

been designed. A well-known example is the sousaphone: a 'circular tuba' with an enormous, forward-facing bell, which is often made of a lighter, synthetic material to save weight.

On your shoulder
You can also get trumpet-shaped euphoniums, horns, and mellophones, and tubas that are designed so that you can rest them on your left shoulder, making them easier to march with. The bells of these instruments point forwards instead of upwards, so the sound is projected toward the audience. Some companies make *convertible* instruments: You switch from an upright tuba to a marching instrument by removing the valve section, turning the instrument around, and reinstalling the valves section.

Without valves
Instruments without valves can play harmonics only. They're referred to as natural instruments (see pages 4 and 100). Some examples are the *natural trumpet* or *clarion*, the *hunting horn*, and the *bugle*. You see such instruments in army bands, for instance, and of course in drum & bugle corps. (*Regulation*) bugles may have one or more slides or valves.

Bach
Valveless instruments are also used in concert halls. When Bach (1685–1750) wrote the Second Brandenburg Concerto, valves hadn't been invented yet – and some musicians choose to play this work on the traditional valveless *baroque trumpet* or *Bach trumpet*.

And what about the sax?
You'd think a saxophone was a brasswind instrument, with its brass tube that gets progressively wider. However, instead of valves, saxophones a have key mechanism, like clarinets and flutes; sthe mouthpiece is also taken from the clarinet. So, although it is a wind instrument made of brass, the sax belongs to the *woodwind* family – like the flute, in fact, even though that instrument is almost always made of metal.

12. HOW THEY'RE MADE

Some companies still make their instruments almost entirely by hand; others leave most of the work to computer-controlled machines. Here's a quick look at some of the processes used in the production of brass instruments.

Most higher-priced instruments have one-piece bells, made of a single sheet of brass. The sheet is cut precisely to size and folded double, after which the seam is soldered.

Hammers
Tipcode TRP-020

Traditionally, wooden hammers are used to hammer the bell in shape against a steel mandrel. To make hammering the brass easier, it is first rolled in a mill. The resulting shape roughly resembles a run-over tulip. In some factories, the hand-hammering has been taken over by machines.

Two parts

The widest part (the flare) of a two-piece bell is made by pressing a small, fast-spinning brass disc in shape against a mandrel, using a tool which very closely resembles a baseball bat. New welding techniques (plasma welding) can make two-piece bells behave like they were seamless, one-piece bells.

The bends

To prevent the tubes from kinking when they are bent, they are first filled. In the past, molten lead would be used. Today it's more likely to be sand, or a soap solution which is frozen inside the tube.

A two-piece bell before assembly.

A flat sheet of brass
(1), folded (2), rolled (3), roughly hammered into shape (4), bent, and finished
(5) (Kanstul).

Bullets

Shorter bend tubes, like the second valve slide, are made perfectly round on the inside by forcing steel balls through them.

By hand

Traditionally, valves and pistons are assembled by hand, one at a time. A single piston is made out of four tubes: the piston itself and the three ports that run through it.

Fit

Before the instrument is finished, all the sliding parts must be made to fit precisely. The more expensive the instrument, the lower the tolerances: a tighter fit, while still running smoothly. Pistons and slides are often hand-lapped for this purpose.

Assembly

Finally the instrument is buffed to a shine and lacquered or plated, assembled, checked, and shipped. Lacquered instruments are usually baked to increase the hardness of the finish.

Lathe

Mouthpieces are made largely on a lathe. The mouthpiece itself turns and a sharp blade takes away the metal that has to be removed. Sometimes the chisel is guided by hand, but usually a computer does this job.

13. BRANDS

There are dozens of companies making brass instruments – from one-man workshops to large factories. This chapter introduces you to the main brand names[1], as well as to some of the lesser-known companies.

Most of the larger, well-known companies produce all four of the instruments covered in this book, as well as other brasswinds, in most price ranges. Some of them also make instruments or parts for other brands. This chapter starts with those companies, followed by an introduction to a number of generally smaller companies, which often focus on a specific price range.

Vincent Bach® The Austrian trumpet player and engineer Vincent Bach made his first mouthpieces in 1918 after moving to New York. About six years later he built his first trumpet. Today, the Bach name is used on a wide variety of brass instruments and accessories.

KING® **C.G. Conn®** **BENGE®** The brands named after trumpet player Elden Benge, cornetist Charles Conn, and trombonist Thomas King all belong to the American company UMI. Though they're being made in one plant, they're three separate brands, each offering instruments in various price ranges.

---

[1] *Trademarks and/or user names have been used in this book solely to identify the products or instruments discussed. Such use does not identify endorsement by or affiliation with the trademark owner(s).*

GETZEN ® T.J. Getzen opened a repair workshop in New York in 1939. A couple of years later he started making his own horns. The company is still family-owned.

HOLTON ® Frank Holton played the trombone in the band led by John Philip Sousa, who gave his name to the sousaphone. MARTIN ® Holton made his first instruments over a hundred years ago. Today, the company belongs to the Leblanc group. Martin brass instruments come from the same company.

KANSTUL ® Zigmant Kanstul learned his trade *MUSICAL INSTRUMENTS* at the now defunct F. E. Olds Company. Prior to founding his own company in 1981 he also worked for King and Conn.

YAMAHA ® The one-man organ factory founded by Torakusu Yamaha in 1889 is now the world's biggest producer of musical instruments, from brasswinds to guitars and drums – and the Japanese company also makes motorbikes, hi-fi equipment, and much more.

More US brands

There are many American brasswind companies. Some of them focus on professional instruments only, their prices starting around two, three, or even five thousand dollars. Well-known names are **Calicchio** (from California), **Edwards** (Edward Getzen, of the Getzen family), **Marcinkiewicz** (makes mouthpieces too), **Monette** (also active in the ten-grand-and-up price range), and **Schilke** (makes mouthpieces too). Other American makers choose to concentrate on affordable instruments, like the family-owned company **Blessing**, or **Burbank**. Some examples of American brands that have their affordably priced instruments (largely) made elsewhere are **Antigua Winds**, **L.A. Horn** (related to the colorful L.A. Saxophones), and **E.M. Winston**.

Asia

Two of the better-known Asian brand names are **Jupiter**

and **Dixon**, both mainly supplying instruments in the lower and middle price ranges. Asian companies often produce 'stencil instruments' too – instruments that are give a brand name by the distributor.

Germany

Most European brass instrument manufacturers can be found in Germany, where many companies specialize in background brasswinds – but they make trumpets and other horns as well. **B&S Challenger**, **VMI**, and **Scherzel** are three brands that come from the same factory. **Alexander**, best known for its French horns, makes a flugelhorn/ trumpet combination as well. Some other examples are **Glassl**, **Kühnl & Hoyer**, and **Miraphone**.

Other European companies

Antoine **Courtois** (known for the Evolution trumpet, but active in all price ranges), **Couesnon**, and **Selmer** (best-known for their saxes; makes professional trumpets and cornets too) are from France. Besson originally came from France, but later moved to England. The French Besson series are made in the US. **Stomvi**, from Spain, also produces combination mouthpieces and titanium 'brass' winds. The Swiss **Willson** company makes flugelhorns, and trombones with their own Rotax valves. **Taylor** brasswinds are hand-made in England. The Czech **Amati** company has budget and mid-range woodwinds and brasswinds. **Cerveny**, focusing on background brass, is a brand name of the same company. **Van Laar**, from the Netherlands, makes professional trumpets and flugelhorns.

And more...

Some of the other brand names you may come across are **Belmonté**, **Capri**, **DEG**, **Ganter**, and **Lazer** – brands that usually have limited catalogs. Two American brand names from the past are **Elkhart** and **Bundy**, which were mainly used for budget instruments of the Bach company.

14. ORCHESTRAS AND BANDS

As a horn player, there are all kinds of bands, orchestras, ensembles, and other lineups you can choose to play in. Here's a short introduction to some of the main groups you can join.

Of course, brasswinds are essential in all the various types of high school and college bands: marching bands that perform either onstage, in parades, or during football games; pep bands, which often also feature a set drummer and an electric bass guitar; wind bands, with brasswinds and woodwinds, including oboes and bassoons; or concert bands, which may have some sixty to more than a hundred band members. A concert band lineup includes all the brasswinds (soprano and background brass), woodwinds (flute, saxophones, clarinets, oboes, and so on), and a traditional percussion setup.

Brass bands and more
As a brass player, you can also join a brass band, of course (the cornet plays an important role here), or a drum & bugle corps, or a community band. If you want brass only, there are brass choirs, and you may also want to join a trombone choir or a trumpet choir. Choirs often play classical or contemporary music, either specifically composed for or adapted to the lineup. Other brasswind ensembles may consist of two trumpets, two French horns, and two or three trombones; or four trumpets, three trombones, and a bass trombone. Brasswind quintets have various lineups: Two trumpets, one trombone, a French horn, and tuba is just one example.

Symphony orchestra

The biggest classical orchestra, the symphony orchestra, may contain over a hundred musicians. The violinists are the largest group. Larger orchestras often have five trumpet players and three or four trombonists, along with other brass players (French horn, tuba, and so on), woodwind players (flute, clarinet, etc.), percussionists, harpists, and a pianist. Chamber orchestras are much smaller.

Other formats

Classical music – and many other styles of music as well – can be played in numerous other lineups, which perform compositions that were written specifically for or adapted to the instruments used. Some examples include works for one, two, or three brasswinds with piano, or with strings and harpsichord, or with tympani only, or with an equal number of violins, or works for solo trumpet and solo voice, or an ensemble that consists of trumpet, two violins, flute, and French horn...

Jazz

The cornet was especially popular in the first jazz bands, which sprang up in the early 1900s. You still find them in Dixieland bands. Later, the trumpet gained the upper hand. A mainstream or bebop jazz quintet usually consists of a trumpet player, a saxophonist, a pianist, a bassist, and a drummer. Most big bands have four trumpeters, four trombonists, several saxophonists, and of course a pianist, a bassist, and a drummer. High school and college jazz bands may have even more instrumentalists.

Funk and rock

Horn players may feature in all kinds of other popular bands, supplying fancy lines, colorful accents, and sizzling riffs. A typical wind section, with two saxophonists, a trumpeter, and a trombonist, may play any style from jazz dance to salsa, from soul to African pop...

International folk music

... or you can join one of the many ensembles that play the folk music of different countries and cultures, ranging from Mexican mariachi bands to German-oriented polka bands and Jewish klezmer groups, and so on...

GLOSSARY AND INDEX

This glossary contains short definitions of all brasswind-related terms used in this book. There are also some words you won't find on the previous pages, but which you might well come across in magazines, catalogs, and books. The numbers refer to the pages where the term is used in this Tipbook.

Alto trombone *(22)* Higher pitched, smaller trombone in E–flat.

American cornet *(12)* The American cornet is longer than the British or European cornet.

Bach trumpet See: *Piccolo* trumpet.

Backbore See: *Mouthpiece.*

Background brass *(105–109)* Generally low-pitched brass instruments that are mostly used to accompany the melody instruments. Examples are euphoniums, mellophones, baritones, and alto horns. See also: *Soprano brass.*

Bass trombone *(51)* Often has two valves. Mostly the same dimensions as a tenor trombone, but with an extra large bore and bell.

Bell, bell section *(7, 9, 13, 34, 37–38)* The material and taper of the bell section are important to the sound. Some trumpets have a tunable bell.

Bell stay *(14, 15)* The brace in the bell section of a trombone.

B-flat instruments *(16–18)* The most widely-used trumpet is the B-flat trumpet. If you play a C, you will hear a concert B-flat. Most cornets and flugelhorns are

B-flat instruments too, but these *transposing instruments* come in other keys as well *(102)*. Tenor trombones, though pitched in B-flat as well, are not considered transposing instruments *(18)*.

Booster *(71–72)* Metal cap which adds weight to your mouthpiece.

Bore *(10, 34–37, 39, 60, 70, 103)* The bore refers to the size or shape of the inside of a tube. A wide tube has a large bore, a narrow tube has a small bore. A straight tube has a *cylindrical bore*, a tube which gets steadily wider has a *conical bore*. A trombone is largely cylindrical, a flugelhorn is largely conical.

Bottom spring, bottom-sprung See: *Top spring, top-sprung*.

Brass *(32, 34)* An alloy made of a lot of copper and rather less zinc which is the material most commonly used for 'brass' instruments.

British cornet See: *American cornet*.

Bugle *(11, 101, 109)* One of the *natural instruments*, a bugle is like a flugelhorn without valves.

Cases and gig bags *(84–86)* No instrument can do without good protection.

Conical See: *Bore*.

Convertible trombone *(51)* A trombone with a detachable F-attachment. See also: *F-attachment*.

Cornet, Cornet à pistons *Cornet à pistons* or even *piston* is an older name for the short, British cornet.

Crook Bend or bow. See: *Tuning slide*.

C–trumpet *(17–18, 46)* Slightly smaller than the 'regular' B–flat trumpet. See: *B–flat instrument*.

Cup *(61–62, 66–68)* The cup–shaped part of the mouthpiece, within which your lips vibrate.

Cylinder, cylinder valve See: *Valve*.

Cylindrical See: *Bore*.

Dual bore *(36)* A dual bore trombone has a slide with two different bores. Some trumpets come with a dual bore too.

Embouchure *(20, 44)* Your embouchure or 'lip' is your way of playing and your use of lips, jaws and all the muscles around them.

F–attachment *(50–52)* A tube and valve assembly which lowers the pitch of a trombone by a fourth.

Finger buttons *(7, 8, 47)* You operate the valves with the finger buttons.

Fluegelhorn Alternative spelling for flugelhorn.

French style slides *(11)* Vertical valve slides, as used on most flugelhorns.

German trumpet See: *Valves*.

Gig bag *(84–85)* Reinforced bag.

Gooseneck *(49)* The first piece of tubing of a trombone's bell section.

Handgrip *(13)* The inner-slide brace or inner brace on a trombone.

Harmonic *(4, 109)* The notes you can play without using the valves are called harmonics. *Natural instruments* have no valves and can play only harmonics.

Independent, in-line *(51)* On bass-trombones with in-line or independent

rotary valves, the valves can be used independently from each other. If the valves are *stacked* or *offset*, they can't.

Inner slide, outer slide See: *Slide*.

Insurance *(88, 130–131)* Smart move.

Intonation *(53–55, 57, 83)* The better the intonation of an instrument, the easier it is to play it in tune.

Lacquer *(32–33)* Most modern brass instruments are lacquered. Some are silver- or gold-plated instead *(32, 33)*. Occasionally, you will find nickel-plated instruments too *(33)*.

Lapping *(28, 112)* Polishing parts for a perfect fit.

Leadpipe *(7, 8, 39–40)* Also called *mouthpipe*: the piece of tubing between the mouthpiece receiver and the tuning slide.

Lip See: *Embouchure*.

Low brass *(105–109)* Low brass includes lower pitched instruments such as baritones and tubas.

Lyre, lyre holder *(10)* (Clamp for) holder of sheet music.

Lyre with click-on system for lyre holder.

Main tuning slide See: *Tuning slide.*

Microphones *(87)* Handy if you need to play at high volume.

Monel *(47)* Copper/nickel alloy, often used for valves.

Mouthpiece *(6, 7, 55, 57, 61–73, 95, 97)* Important for your technique and how comfortably you play. Dimensions to take into account are: the size and depth of the *cup (66–68)*, the width and shape of the *rim (68–70)*, the smallest opening *(bore* or *throat; 70)* and the shape and size of the *backbore* (the inside of the *shank,* the part of the mouthpiece which fits into the mouthpiece receiver of your instrument; *71).*

Mouthpiece receiver See: *Receiver.*

Mouthpipe See: *Leadpipe.*

Mute *(74–77)* Most mutes

fit into the bell of your instrument. Practice mutes really do mute the sound; other mutes are mainly for effects.

Natural instrument *(4, 100, 109) Natural instruments* have no valves and can only play harmonics. They are also known as *signal instruments.* See also: *Harmonic.*

Nickel silver *(45–46)* Alloy of copper, zinc, nickel, and some other metals – but no silver. Also known as German silver, white bronze or alpaca.

Offset See: *Independent, in-line.*

Outer slide, inner slide See: *Slide.*

Pedal note A confusing term, as you can gather from the following four statements: *'Pedal notes are fundamentals'; 'Pedal notes are the very lowest notes* *you can play on a brass instrument'; 'Since getting my new mouthpiece, I've been able to blow a pedal-C on my trumpet'; 'You can't play pedal notes on a trumpet'.* One conclusion: Pedal notes are very low notes. On an organ you really would play them with the pedals.

Périnet valves See: *Valves.*

Piccolo trumpet *(102)* Small, very high-sounding trumpet with four valves. Also called *Bach trumpet.*

reduces the volume of your instrument.

Receiver *(7, 8, 46)* The tube you stick your mouthpiece into. Also called *Venturi tube.*

Reversed leadpipe, reversed tuning slide *(39)* The tuning slide slides over the leadpipe, rather than into it, creating a smoother airflow.

Rim See: *Mouthpiece.* Also refers to the edge of the bell.

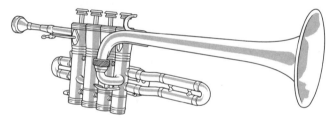

Piccolo trumpet.

Piston, piston valves See: *Cornet à pistons* and *Valves.*

Piston guides *(46, 47)* Make for accurate port alignment. Also known as *valve guides.*

Pocket trumpet *(103, 108)* Very tightly 'rolled-up' trumpet; sounds the same pitch as a regular trumpet.

Practice mute *(23–24)* A type of mute which greatly

Rotary instrument *(50, 103–104)* Instrument with *rotary valves* or *rotors.* See: *Valves.*

Rotary valve, rotor See: *Valves.*

Shank See: *Mouthpiece.*

Shepherd's crook *(12)* On the short, British cornet, the double bend after the valves has the shape of a shepherd's crook.

Silver plating *(32–33, 57)* Instead of lacquer, an instrument may be silver-plated or even gold-plated. These precious metals will last longer than lacquer will. Virtually all mouthpieces are silver-plated, but gold-plated mouthpieces are also available *(72)*.

Slide *(4, 5, 13, 14, 36, 48, 59–60, 80, 94)* The slide or *hand slide* of a trombone consists of an *inner slide* (with two tubes) and a moveable *outer slide*. You hold the inner slide with the *inner slide brace* or *inner brace* and you work the outer slide with the *outer brace* or *slide stay*. At the two ends, the inner tube gets slightly thicker. These thickened ends are referred to as the *stockings*. See also: *Valve slides*.

Slide lock *(14, 59–60)* Stops a trombone slide moving of its own accord.

Slide stop *(44)* Prevents a (third) valve slide from slipping off.

Slide trumpet *(100)* Old-fashioned trumpet; incorrect name for the trombone.

Soprano brass *(105)* Brass instruments can be divided in soprano brass, which includes the higher sounding horns (trumpets, cornets, etc.), and low brass (trombone, tuba, euphonium, etc.). See also: *Background brass*.

Spit valve See: *Water key.*

Stacked See: *Independent, in-line.*

Stockings *(48)* Thicker sections at the ends of a trombone slide's inner tubes.

Straight bore See: *Dual bore.*

Straight trombone *(51)* Trombone without (F-) attachment.

Tenor trombone *(13)* The most popular trombone; comes with or without F-attachment. See also: *F-attachment.*

Throat See: *Mouthpiece.*

Top action, top spring *(46–47)* On most piston-type valves, the spring is above the piston (*top action* or *top spring*). On a bottom-sprung valve it is underneath the piston (*bottom spring*).

Transposing instruments See: *B-flat instruments.*

Trigger *(11, 45)* Mechanism to operate the valve slide(s) on a flugelhorn. Sometimes used on trumpets and cornets too.

Trim *(33)* Replaceable parts, *i.e.*, valve stems, finger buttons, top and bottom valve caps, and so on.

Tuning bell, tunable bell See: *Bell.*

Tuning crook See: T*uning slide.*

Tuning slide *(7, 8, 10, 12, 39, 40, 80–82)* You tune a flugelhorn with the tuning slide, the (straight) section of tubing into which the mouthpiece fits. Trumpets, cornets and trombones are tuned with the U-shaped tuning slide or *main tuning slide,* also known as (*main*) *tuning crook.*

Valves *(4, 6, 7, 46–48, 58, 79–80, 90–92, 100–101)* Valves are used to make the tube

of an instrument longer, lowering the tones it can produce. Most trumpets, cornets, and flugelhorns have *piston valves* or *Périnet valves* that work with a *piston,* moving up and down. The main part of a *rotary valve, rotor,* or *cylinder valve,* which can be found on trombones *(50, 59, 93)* and rotary trumpets *(German trumpets; 103– 104),* among other horns, makes a rotating movement. The group of valves on an instrument is referred to as *valve section, valve cluster,* or *valve block.*

Valve casing *(8, 97)* Each piston is enclosed in its own valve casing.

Valve guide See: *Piston guide.*

Valve slides *(7, 8, 11, 43–45, 90–92, 98)* U-shaped pieces of tubing attached to the valves; also referred to as *slides.*

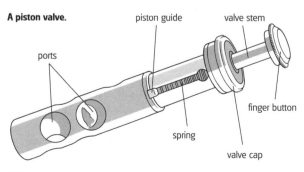

A piston valve.

piston guide

valve stem

ports

finger button

spring

valve cap

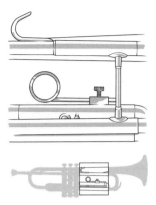

An adjustable finger ring on the third valve slide.

Valved trombone *(53)* Trombone with piston valves and no slide, like a trumpet.

Venturi tube See: *Receiver.*

Water key *(7, 10, 41, 58, 59)* Water keys allow you to remove the condensation that collects in your instrument. They're also known as spit valves.

Wrap *(51)* Trombones with one or two valves may have an *open wrap,* in which the extra tubing of the attachment(s) sticks out behind the instrument, or a *closed* or *traditional wrap,* in which it stays inside the bell section. See also: *F-attachment.*

TIPCODE LIST

The Tipcodes in this book offer easy access to short movies, photo series, soundtracks, and other additional information at www.tipbook.com. For your convenience, the Tipcodes in this Tipbook have been listed below.

Tipcode	Topic	Chapter	Page
TRP-001	Trumpet and trombone	1	1
TRP-002	Trumpet and flugelhorn	1	1
TRP-003	Harmonics	2	4
TRP-004	Second valve	2	5
TRP-005	Trigger	2	11
TRP-006	Trombone slide	2	13
TRP-007	Depressing a valve	5	46
TRP-008	Testing hand slide	5	59
TRP-009	Straight mute	7	74
TRP-010	Cup mute	7	75
TRP-011	Harmon mute	7	75
TRP-012	Plunger	7	76
TRP-013	Assembling a trombone	8	78
TRP-014	A=440	8	81
TRP-015	Tuning fork	8	81
TRP-016	Tuning (tuning slide)	8	82
TRP-017	440 vs 442	8	83
TRP-018	Lubricating a rotor	9	91
TRP-019	Removing valve slide with cloth	9	98
TRP-020	How they're made	12	110

WANT TO KNOW MORE?

This Tipbook gives you all the basic information you need for buying, maintaining, and using a trumpet, trombone, flugelhorn, or cornet. If you want to know more, you can consult the magazines, books, and websites listed below.

MAGAZINES

This list includes the main magazines for brass players.

- *Band & Orchestra Product News*, phone (516) 767-2500, www.bandandorchestra.com.
- *ITG Journal*, fax (413) 568-1913, www.trumpetguild.org (published by the International Trumpet Guild (ITG).
- *Windplayer*, phone (310) 456-5813, www.windplayer.com.
- *The Brass Player*, fax (212) 581-1480, www.charlescolin.com.
- *Brass Bulletin* (Swiss; also published in English), phone +41 (0)21 909-1000, www.brass-bulletin.ch.
- *Brass Band World* (UK), phone +44 (0)129 881-2816, www.brassbandworld.com.
- *British Bandsman* (UK; weekly), phone +44 (0)149 467-4411, www.britishbandsman.com.

BOOKS

The following is a brief selection of brasswind books that cover some of the subjects of this Tipbook in greater depth.

- *A Complete Guide to Brass Instruments and Techniques*, by Scott Whitener (Schirmer Books, 1997; 380 pages; ISBN 0 028 64597 9).
- *The Cambridge Companion to Brass Instruments*, edited by Trevor Herbert and John Wallace (Cambridge

University Press, 1997; 325 pages; ISBN 0 521 56522 7).
- *20th Century Brass Musical Instruments in the United States*, by Richard J. Dundas (Honeybee Health Products, 1998; 88 pages; ISBN 0 961 70931 6).
- *The Complete Guide to Trumpet Playing (For Classical and Jazz Musicians)*, by Garree Stephan (Stephan Publications, 2000; ISBN 1884524222).
- *The Sax & Brass Book: Saxophones, Trumpets and Trombones in Jazz, Rock and Pop*, by Tony Bacon (Backbeat Books, 1998; 120 pages; ISBN 0 879 30531 2).
- *The Trombonist's Handbook: a Complete Guide to Playing and Teaching the Trombone*, Reginald H. Fink (Accura Music, Ohio, 1970/1977; 145 pages; ISBN 0 918194 01 6).
- *Brass Instruments: Their History and Development*, by Anthony Baines (Dover Publications, 1993; 300 pages; ISBN 0 486 27574 4).
- *Comparative Mouthpiece Guide for Trumpet*, by Gerald Endsley (Tromba Publications, 1992; ISBN unknown).

INTERNET

On the Internet, you'll find countless sites for brass players, often with all kinds of links, articles, discussion groups, and FAQs (Frequently Asked Questions – and their answers). The following sites are good starting points for your search. Also check the websites mentioned above. Please note that website addresses are subject to change.
- Brass Resources: www.whc.net/rjones/brassrsc.html.
- Flugelhorn Knowledge Base: www.flugelhorn.com.
- The Flugelhorn Society: www.geocities.com/Vienna/8361.
- The International Trombone Association: www.ita-web.org.
- TromboneFAQ: www.brusseau.com/TromboneFAQ.
- The International Trumpet Guild: www.trumpetguild.org/links/links.htm.
- The Trumpet Herald: www.trumpetherald.com.
- Trumpet Player Online: www.v-zone.com/tpo
- Trumpet Players' International Network: www.tpin.org.

ABOUT THE MAKERS

Journalist, writer and musician Hugo Pinksterboer, (co)author of the Tipbook Series, has published hundreds of interviews, articles, and instrument, video, CD, and book reviews for national and international music magazines. He wrote the reference work for cymbals (*The Cymbal Book*) and has written and developed a wide variety of manuals and courses, both for musicians and non-musicians.

Illustrator, designer, and musician Gijs Bierenbroodspot was art director for a wide variety of magazines, and has developed numerous ad campaigns. While searching for information about saxophone mouthpieces, he got the idea for this series of books. He is responsible for the layout and the illustrations for all of the Tipbooks. He has also found a good mouthpiece, in the meantime.

ESSENTIAL DATA

In the event of your instrument being stolen or lost, or if you decide to sell it, it's useful to have all the relevant data at hand. Here are two pages to list everything you need – for the insurance, for the police, or just for yourself.

INSURANCE

Company:

Phone: Fax:

E-mail:

Agent:

Phone: Fax:

E-mail:

Policy number: Premium:

INSTRUMENTS AND ACCESSORIES

Brand and type:

Serial number:

Price:

Date of purchase:

Purchased from:

Phone: Fax:

Brand and type:

Serial number:

Price:

Date of purchase:

Purchased from:

Phone: Fax:

Brand and type:

Serial number:

Price:

Date of purchase:

Purchased from:

Phone: Fax:

Brand and type:

Serial number:

Price:

Date of purchase:

Purchased from:

Phone: Fax:

ADDITIONAL NOTES

....

....

....

....

....

....

....

....

....

....

....

....

....

....

....

....

....

....

....

....

ADDITIONAL NOTES